HEALING THE INNER CHILD

A Guided Journal

By Inward Companion

Copyright © 2024
ISBN 979-8-218-46475-2

Thank You for Your Support

This journal is our heartfelt effort to be of service.

We would truly love to hear your feedback, requests, and thoughts. Drop us a note on social media @inwardcompanion or email us at inwardcompanion@gmail.com.

If you found this book helpful, please help us spread the word. Write a review, share a picture or video of your journal on TikTok or Instagram, and tag @inwardcompanion.

Send your review or video link to inwardcompanion@gmail.com or @inwardcompanion, and we'll send you special bonus content as a thank you.

Follow @inwardcompanion on Instagram or TikTok, or join our email list to stay updated on new releases and materials.

Important Note

It's crucial to note that while this book offers insights and guidance, it is not a replacement for professional mental health advice. If you are struggling with severe mental health issues, we strongly encourage you to seek support from qualified professionals. Their care can be vital for navigating such challenges.

If at any point you feel too overwhelmed or triggered, stop reading immediately and consult a mental health provider. Please note that the authors and publishers are not liable for any adverse effects resulting from the use of this book.

Legal Liability Statement:

This book is intended for informational purposes only and is not a substitute for professional advice or treatment. While every effort has been made to ensure the accuracy and completeness of the information provided, we make no representations or warranties of any kind, express or implied, about the completeness, accuracy, reliability, suitability, or availability with respect to the contents of this book.

The authors, publishers, and contributors of this book shall not be liable for any direct, indirect, consequential, incidental, special, or exemplary damages arising out of the use of the information contained in this book or reliance on any information provided herein.

Readers are advised to consult with appropriate professionals for specific advice tailored to their individual circumstances. Any reliance you place on the information contained in this book is strictly at your own risk. We disclaim any responsibility for any loss or damage, including without limitation, indirect or consequential loss or damage, or any loss or damage whatsoever arising from loss of data or profits arising out of, or in connection with, the use of this book.

Table of Content

Acknowledgment

Our heartfelt gratitude goes to those who have supported us on our inner child journey and whose work we have referenced. Your guidance and love have been invaluable. This book would not have been possible without you.

Natalie Y Gutierrez
Author, Complex Trauma Therapist, Healer
www.natalieygutierrez.com

Monika Wyss
Systemic Therapist and Family Constellation Trainer
www. heartsanctuary.center

Phoebe Yee
American Certified Marriage and Family Therapist
www.heartin-therapy.com

Dedication

This book is dedicated to our late fathers. May you rest in peace. We imagine how beautiful it would have been if you had received the love, support, and care you needed as a child. Out of that wish, we wrote this book.

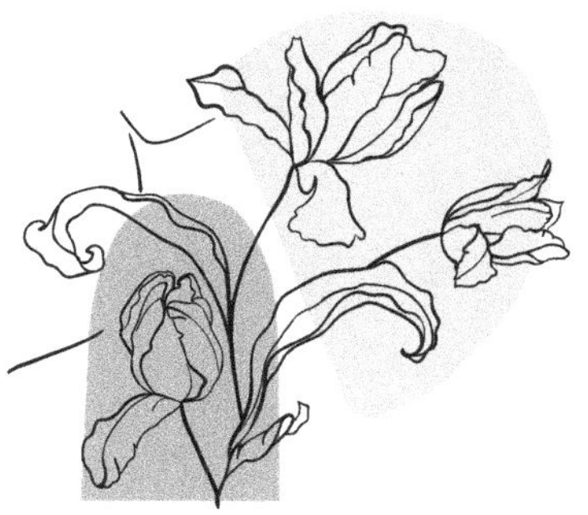

About the Authors

We are two creatives who once carried deeply wounded inner children. Through our own unique journeys, we found ways to comfort and tend to these inner parts. Now we hope to help you, our readers, do the same, as your companions on this path inward.

After years of therapy, inner work and various healing modalities, our paths crossed at a 10-day silent meditation retreat. Inspired to share the knowledge, tools, and wisdom we wished we had in our younger years, we embarked on this journey to be of service. This book is our heartfelt offering, written with the hope that it will support you in your own inner child journey. We are honored to walk this path with you.

"The inner child is the gateway to discovering our True Self – to reconnecting with the Great Spirit."

– Robert Burney

# Introduction

"But it made you stronger."

I was a child
I didn't need to be stronger
I needed to be safe.

- Fran Mullins

Welcome & Introduction to the Journal

If you're reading this, chances are you have been feeling unwell. Maybe most of the time. It's like something's not right, but you can't quite put your finger on it. You've felt numb, empty, maybe even sad at times, without really knowing why. And you're tired of feeling this way.

You want to feel better, but you're not sure where to start. You might have tried chasing after certain goals, thinking they would finally bring you the peace, joy, and love you have been craving. Whether it was money, looks, love, fame, or success, you hoped that achieving these goals would fill the void inside. But those external achievements don't provide lasting fulfillment.

Even if you reach them, the satisfaction fades quickly, and you're left with the same underlying discomfort. Why? Because the real source of your suffering lies within. Deep emotional wounds, many of which were formed during your childhood, are still hurting you. Over the years, these wounds have piled up, buried deep within you. You've developed coping mechanisms and even entire personas to avoid facing them. But ignoring them only makes things worse, amplifying your pain. That's where this book comes in.

This book is a simple guide to help you begin to explore, understand, and soothe those past hurts. We'll introduce you to foundational concepts of the mind and the inner child, showing you how they influence your life. Then, we'll walk you through a process of healing and reparenting your wounded inner child.

We'll also guide you to dive deeper and uncover other parts of yourself that need healing. Finally, we'll show you how to reconnect with the joyful, authentic parts of your inner child —the parts that still want to play, enjoy life, and feel alive. We'll be using the language of our inner child -- our imagination and our creativity -- to embark on this journey together. So let's dive in and start.

"It's important for people to know that no matter what lies in their past, they can overcome the dark side and press on to a brighter world."

— Dave Pelzer

How You Should Approach the Journal:

Approaching inner work can feel overwhelming or intimidating, so remember to take your time and be gentle with yourself.

Inner health is a lifelong journey and a lifestyle.

How would you like to commit to yourself?

I can commit to _________________ minutes per day

for _________________ days per week.

And don't forget, it's okay to recommit and start over as many times as needed. Like a caring parent, find a balance between being too hard on yourself and being too lenient.

Prioritize self-care throughout this process. It may feel challenging, but know that it will be worth it.

Healing is NOT linear

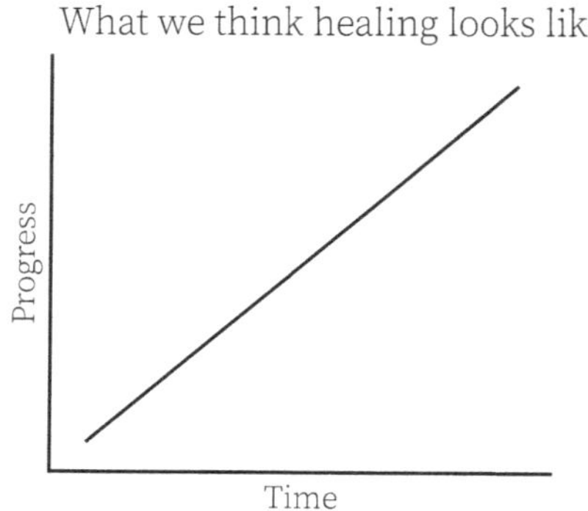

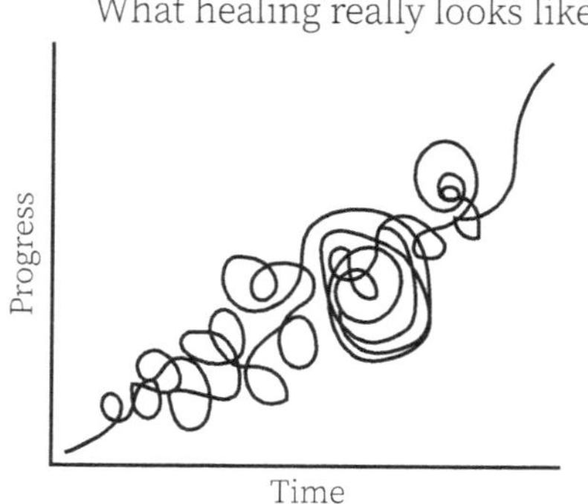

Important Reminder

As you embark on this journey, you might find yourself confronting extremely challenging emotions that were once too much to handle. But now, you may be in a place where you're ready to face them and learn how to be with them. But like acquiring any new skill, it can be challenging and awkward in the beginning.

During this process, it's crucial to be compassionate and patient with yourself. Just like you can't force a baby to stop crying, you can't rush through these tough experiences. Instead, you can offer yourself love and support, allowing those emotions to pass through in their own time.

Remember to take plenty of breaks when you need them, and to come back when you're ready. There's no rush or deadline — inner work is a lifelong practice, and it's okay to take it one step at a time.

Background

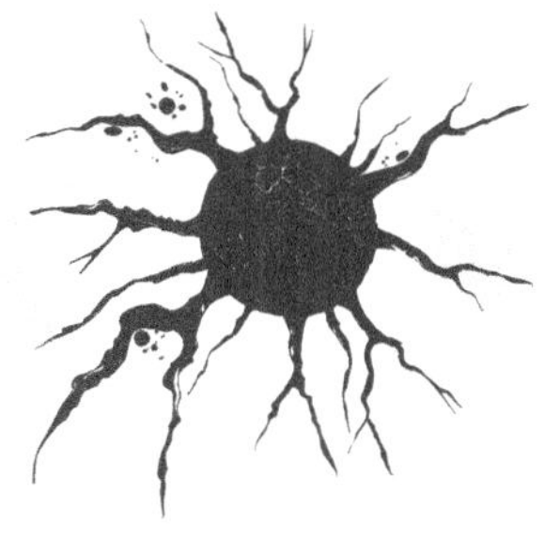

What Are Inner Child Wounds?

Our early experiences, especially from ages 0 to 7, shape who we become as adults. Inner child wounds form when children face overwhelming emotional experiences without adequate support, leaving them alone with feelings of hurt and shame.

To cope, children repress painful experiences, develop protective strategies, and distract themselves. Each unresolved experience creates an inner child fragment, forming a network of wounded emotional selves.

Understanding Behaviorism

Many modern parenting techniques are rooted in "behaviorism," where parents shape a child's behavior through rewards and consequences. While often done out of love, this approach can have harmful impacts. For example, animals generally do not ignore their crying young, as the cries often signal hunger, discomfort, or danger. But many parents today are advised to ignore their crying children to "cry it out".

The Impact on Children

When ignored, children may stop crying, but their needs remain unmet. They may internalize feelings of abandonment, leading to a fear of being left alone and a desperate constant seeking for care. Some children may develop hyper-independence and distrust of caregivers, entering survival mode and doubting their safety. This is one example of how inner child wounds can form due to unmet needs and unaddressed emotional distress.

Emotional wounds from our childhood shape our thoughts, behaviors, and emotions. They are typically at the root of our painful feelings and behavior that we don't understand, like, or know is best for us.

Why Is Inner Child Healing Important?

These coping mechanisms, while initially protective, can hinder our ability to express ourselves, set boundaries, or manage emotions effectively as adults. We might struggle with vulnerability, connection, and fulfillment in relationships and careers due to unresolved childhood issues.

The inner child healing journey is about recognizing, connecting with, and tending to emotional wounds from childhood, ultimately leading to improved emotional regulation, increased self-awareness, and enhanced overall wellbeing.

Imagine encountering a boy whose hand was burnt by fire, cowering in pain and fear after being hurt.

He might have healed the physical wound, but emotionally, he remains traumatized. While the adults around him may have helped heal his physical injury, no one helped him make sense of what happened.

As he grows into adulthood, he develops an extreme protective mechanism, avoiding fire altogether.

Now, envision that he not only heals his physical wound but also understands why he got hurt. He learns from his experience, recognizing the dangerous nature of fire. He understands how to use it as a tool and how to protect himself from getting hurt.

He develops resilience and a sense of safety, gaining an understanding of how to work with fire safely and recognizing when it is unsafe.

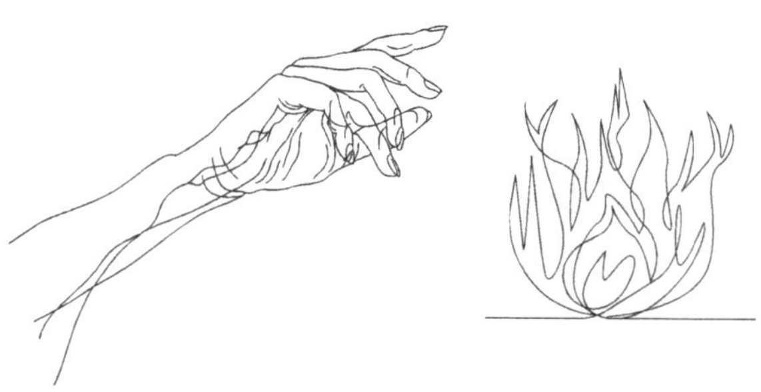

This illustration highlights the importance of acknowledging and tending to our wounded emotions—the hurt, the fear, and the protective mechanisms. When we repress these feelings, they become open wounds. We also don't fully see the nature of the situation and learn how to best navigate the world.

But by allowing ourselves to tap into, experience and process these emotions, we initiate the healing journey. We unravel the layers of pain and protective mechanisms, paving the way for growth and transformation.

Often, as young children in vulnerable situations, our hurtful emotions were not addressed by the people we relied on.

The adults around us lacked the tools and awareness to help with the emotional pain caused by our childhood experiences, likely repeating how they were parented.

By healing our inner child wounds and re-parenting ourselves, we not only heal ourselves but also gain a valuable skill to pass down through our family lineage.

Taking responsibility for our emotional well-being and actively working to heal empowers us to create a brighter, more compassionate future for ourselves and future generations. **Moreover, it allows us to finally live our best lives.**

"Children don't get traumatized because they are hurt.
They get traumatized because they're alone with the hurt."
-Dr. Gabor Mate

The Brain

At the core of our subconscious mind lies the brain, a marvel of evolutionary design made up of billions of interconnected neurons. This complex neural network orchestrates our thoughts, emotions, and behaviors, shaping our conscious experience. Within the brain, specialized structures like the limbic system, known as the emotional brain, and the prefrontal cortex, responsible for higher cognitive functions, play vital roles.

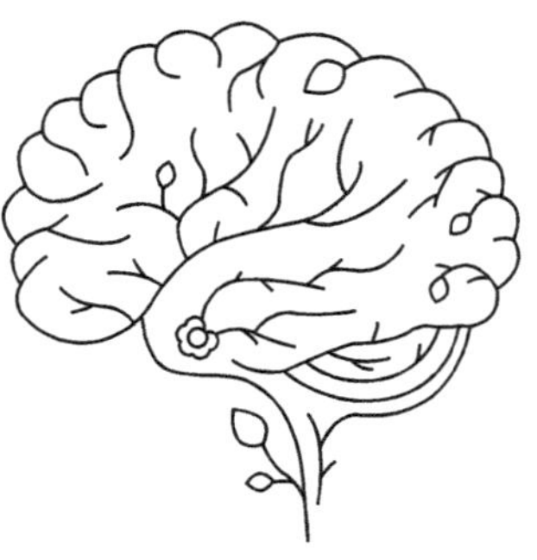

The Amygdala in the Limbic System
The limbic system is a complex set of structures in the brain that deal with emotions and memory. The amygdala, specifically, plays a key role in processing emotions such as fear, anger, and pleasure, and it is also involved in forming and storing memories associated with these emotions.

The Prefrontal Cortex
The prefrontal cortex is located at the front of the brain and is associated with higher cognitive functions. These include decision-making, planning, social behavior, and regulating emotions. It is crucial for complex behaviors, personality expression, and moderating social conduct. It works closely with the limbic system to balance emotional responses with rational thought.

The Inner Child in the Brain
The concept of the "inner child" refers to the part of the psyche that retains the feelings, memories, and experiences of childhood. This inner child can be a source of joy and creativity, but also of unresolved trauma and emotional pain. The amygdala, with its role in processing fear and emotional memories, is often activated by experiences that trigger these unresolved childhood emotions. The prefrontal cortex, which helps in rational thinking and emotional regulation, can help reframe these experiences and provide a more balanced response. The tools in this journal are designed to engage the prefrontal cortex.

The Subconscious Mind

Around 90-95% of our cognitive activities are unconscious, with only 5-10% being conscious. This means most of our thoughts, feelings, and behaviors are driven by the subconscious mind. It controls essential functions like heartbeat and respiration but also stores beliefs and emotional reactions, especially those related to past traumatic experiences.

The subconscious mind is like the hidden part of an iceberg, holding a vast reservoir of memories, beliefs, and emotions. It processes information and influences our responses to the world beyond our awareness. By integrating past experiences with the present, it shapes our perceptions and decisions. The subconscious explains why we are often unaware of the influences from our inner child wounds.

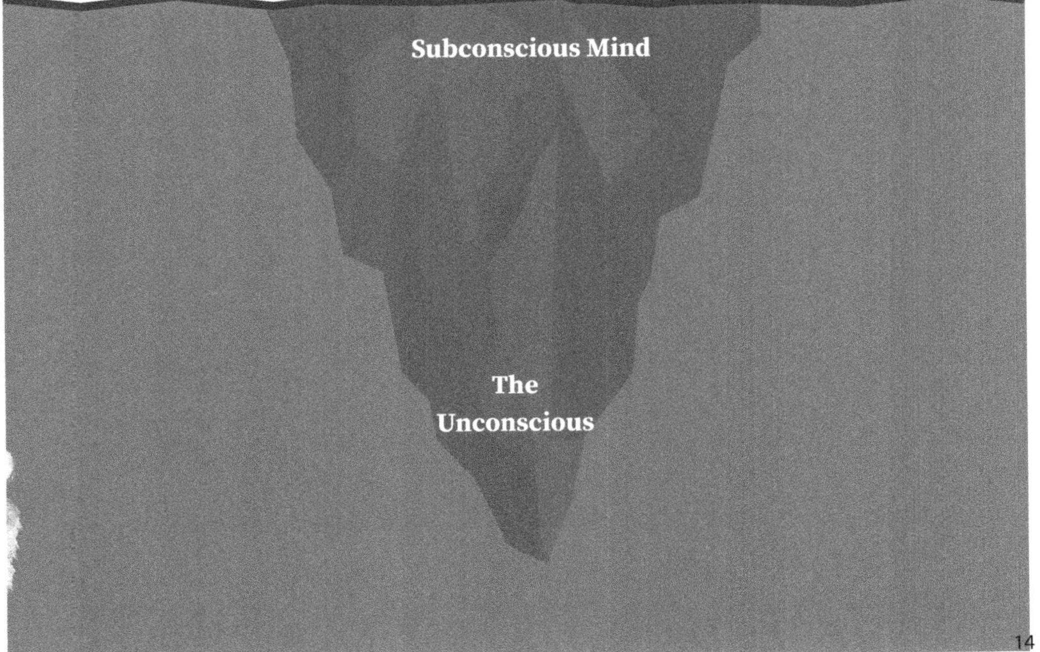

The Internal Family Systems Model

The Internal Family Systems (IFS) model, pioneered by Dr. Richard Schwartz in the 1980s, emerged from his observations in family therapy. IFS helps us approach our subconscious by recognizing that we each have different internal parts, like a team. The mind is a diverse landscape where these parts coexist, each with its own feelings, thoughts, agendas, and actions. Some parts protect us, while others hold past hurts. It's like having a family inside us, where each part has a role, sometimes working together and sometimes not.

In this model, the wounded inner child is typically an "Exiled" part. There isn't just one inner child but many from different stages of our past, such as a terrified 7-year-old, a rebellious 14-year-old, or a neglected 3-year-old. These inner children coexist in our mind.

There are also parts that prevent us from looking at the wounded children, protecting us from the intensity of the pain. Leading this team is the Core Self, our authentic adult self—a compassionate, wise center within us all, orchestrating healing and harmony among these internal parts.

In this journal, we will connect with our Core Self, or our Adult Self/Ideal Parent, as we lead the healing for our wounded inner children.

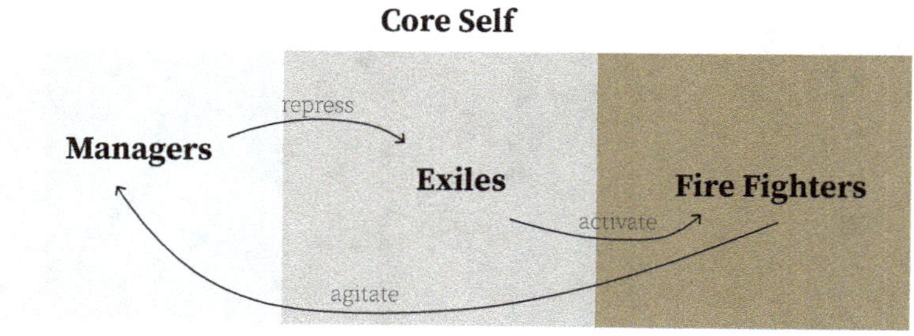

Main Parts in the IFS Model

The following illustrates main parts in the IFS therapy model and their roles.

	Components	Role in the System	IFS Therapy Goals
Core Self	Core Self/ Adult	-Inquisitive, empathetic, imaginative, and self-assured. -In more polarized systems, parts often do not trust the core self's leadership and wisdom.	-Distinguish the core self from other blended parts. -Enhance self-leadership within the system. -Foster inner harmony and reduce polarization among parts.
Exiles	Terrified 7 year old / Ashamed 14 year old	-Carry unacknowledged and painful emotions and trauma memories. -Primarily consist of child and adolescent parts.	-Seek acknowledgment, unburdening, reassurance, and nurturing from the self. -Cease hijacking the system.
Managers	Inner Critic / Angry Protector / The Workholic	-Suppress and confine exiled parts. -Safeguard the system and concentrate on daily activities.	-Release extreme roles. -Adapt roles to present-day needs and operate under the core self's leadership. -Develop greater trust in the core self.
Fire Fighters	Addicts / Depressed Self	-Employ extreme methods to distract, dissociate, and numb the system when exiled parts are triggered.	-No longer need to perform their extreme roles.

"Turns out, in this inner world, you can literally change the past"

-Dr. Richard Schwartz

Somatic Experiencing
The Importance of Feeling Our Feelings

Somatic Experiencing (SE) is a concept developed by Dr. Peter A. Levine to help relieve trauma and chronic stress by focusing on the body's sensations. Unlike processing logically, SE connects the mind and body, making individuals aware of physical sensations linked to past traumas. By gently noticing and allowing these sensations, one releases stored energy and restores the nervous system's natural balance, promoting healing and resilience.

The Gazelle's Lesson: Releasing Stress and Trauma

For example, studies on wild animals, such as gazelles, have shown that after being chased by predators like lions, they often shake their bodies vigorously once they reach safety. This natural shaking helps the gazelle release the built-up stress and return to a calm state, resuming their normal activities, and integrating the survival lessons of the chase.

Humans, however, tend to store stress and trauma in their bodies instead of releasing it. Unlike the gazelle, we often don't have a natural mechanism to shake off the stress, leading to stored tension and trauma.

Somatic Experiencing helps humans release this stored stress by focusing on bodily sensations, allowing us to process and let go of trauma, and return to a state of balance and well-being.

Healing begins with being fully present with your pain. Observe and feel it without resistance, allowing it to express through you. This isn't easy—it takes courage to be with the uncomfortable emotions. But with time and practice, it becomes more natural, a skill you can develop.

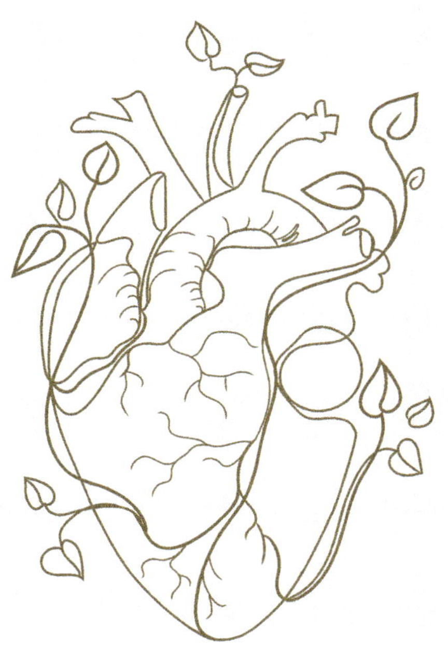

Part 1:
Healing Your Inner Child's Wounds

What is Healing?

> Heal - ing
> *noun*
> The process of making or becoming sound or healthy again.
>
> (Oxford Dictionary)

Our Healing Approach

There are many takes on healing. Our approach is to focus on allowing your inner children to feel safe and secure. It involves:

- **Surfacing Emotional Pain**: Bringing suppressed, repressed, or unconscious emotions to the surface.
- **Soothing and Tending**: Comforting and caring for these emotions, addressing the pain that influences our triggers and behaviors.

The Process

Our healing process involves reparenting ourselves: caring for the neglected and abandoned parts of our inner children. It seems simple, but it requires learning brand new skills to ensure these parts feel safe and secure once more.

How Would We Approach a Scared and Crying Child?

- Be a proactive, calm and caring parent.
- Be patient and hold space for the distress.
- Acknowledge and fully see the distress.
- Understand and soothe the distress to our best ability.
- Let them express emotions they don't understand or know how to handle.
- Teach them to cope with tough emotions and channel them positively.

You are not here to rid yourself of or reject your inner children. Healing isn't about eliminating them or achieving a one-time fix. It's a reparenting process to truly connect with your parts and provide yourself with love and respect. It's about reliably soothing yourself and building a strong, lifelong relationship, much like one would with their own children. A crying child doesn't disappear; they are soothed and continue on with their lives. Often, through this work, the inner children do eventually grow up or find rest, but that's not the main goal.

Why You Need to Reparent Yourself

- You were a child with needs for love, care and safety.
- You didn't get your needs met and that led to an emotional wound.
- You are now an adult in a different environment.
- Only you can finally provide yourself with the love, care, and safety that you needed.

The essence of healing lies in awareness and holding space: making the unconscious conscious and reparenting with our adult self.

Summary

- Healing is about becoming aware of unconscious patterns and painful emotions
- It's about creating a safe space for our emotions, thoughts, and behaviors with compassion and understanding.
- It's about "reparenting" by meeting one's own emotional or physical needs that went unmet in childhood. This could include a lack of emotional support, affection, security, attachment, or structure from one's parents.

Emergency Toolkit for Emotional Distress

If you find yourself in a tough emotional state, PAUSE and take a break. Come back to this page. Find additional professional support if needed.

Your focus is to COREGULATE by being the strong adult who is separate from the distressed inner child, and who can calm down and care for your pain.

Grounding:

Bring yourself back to the present moment, by focusing on sensory experiences and physical sensations.

- Breathe slowly and deeply. Focus on the sensations of your breath in your nose, chest, and throughout your whole body. Feel the sensations of your feet and body on the surface of the floor or furniture.
- Slowly look around your immediate surroundings and name five items you see.
- Slowly look around and name five different colors you observe.
- Label your current location, what you're wearing, and your body sensations.

Refer to page 47 for a more detailed guided breathing exercise.

Taking Breaks and Titrating:

It is important to prioritize self-care when dealing with challenging emotions or situations. Taking space involves recognizing when you need a break or a moment of relaxation and calmness.

- Recognize that it's okay to take breaks when needed, engaging in activities that bring a sense of calm, such as taking a walk or watching TV. You can always come back when you have more energy and emotional capacity.

- Titrating is taking a break in the moment from the pain by shifting your attention from the emotional pain to neutral or positive sensations. For example, focus on a pleasant sensation in your body. When you're ready, gently return to the painful emotion or sensation, only feeling as much as you can tolerate. Move back and forth between these sensations as needed.

Unblending:

Unblend yourself from the overwhelming emotions or inner experiences of your inner child. By unblending, you reconnect with your core adult self and create psychological distance with your inner child's distressing emotions, allowing for clearer observation and understanding.

○ Pay attention to the physical sensations in your heart, grounding yourself in the present.
○ Connect with your present adult self, acknowledging their strength and resilience. Remind yourself that you are no longer a child and that the emotions are not you.
○ Imagine the emotions belong to your inner child. Then:
  ○ Ask your inner child to unblend from you and to not take over.
  ○ Let them know you need space so you can better observe and acknowledge their experience.
  ○ Ask them to reduce the intensity of the emotions down, whether by 25%, 50% or even 99%.
  ○ Let them know that the reduced level would allow you to better support them.

Movement and Discharging Energy:

Emotions are not solely experienced in the mind but can also be felt in the body. It is often said that emotions stand for **energy in motion**. It is then beneficial to find healthy outlets whether through movements, sounds, or physical activities.

○ Accept that feeling physical sensations or the urge to move during emotional processing is normal and should be allowed without judgment. It is normal to yawn, burp, sigh, or sway during the healing process.
○ Allow yourself to discharge pent-up energy through physical movement or other forms of release. Taking a walk outside, dancing, or exercising can be some healthy ways of discharging energy.

"If someone else's reaction seems out of proportion to the situation, it usually means that something else was triggered."

-Dr. Lauren Fogel

Meeting Your
Adult Self

Exercise 1: Connecting with the Ideal Parent

To embark on the journey of healing, we will first connect with and strengthen the ideal parent (aka our adult self or core self). This is the part of you who has always been there within and will be there to reparent our inner child.

For many of us, the ideal parent we longed for wasn't a reality. As we step into the role of reparenting our inner child, we're tasked with becoming the best parent to ourselves. We begin by connecting to the best attributes for our ideal parents.

Slowly read each quality on the next page, one by one. As you review them, imagine an ideal parent embodying each quality.

-   What does it look like for them to demonstrate that quality?
-   How do they interact with you?

Now, take a moment to imagine how it would feel to be in the presence of such a parent. Recognize that these qualities already exist within you, and you have always had access to them. Come back regularly to this exercise to strengthen your ideal parent within.

Qualities of the Ideal Parent

Calm

Serenity regardless of circumstances. The ability to react to triggering situations mindfully.

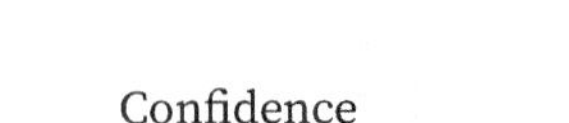

Confidence

The ability to stay fully present in a situation and effectively handle anything that happens. Growth that comes from healing past traumas and an understanding that life includes making mistakes.

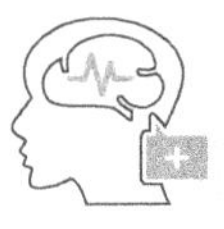

Clarity

The ability to perceive situations clearly, without distortion caused by beliefs. Able to remain objective in situations where you have an interest in the outcome.

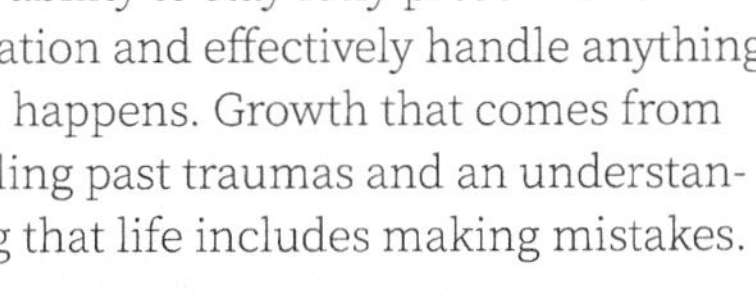

Courage

Having the strength to overcome threats, challenges or danger; taking responsibility for one's actions and being willing to reflect and improve upon the past.

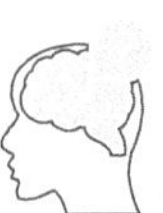

Curiosity

A strong desire to non-judgmentally explore and learn something new about a topic, situation or person. to have a sense of wonder about the world.

Compassion

Being open-hearted, present, and appreciative of others -- without feeling the urge to fix, change distance or judge.

Creativity

A flow state, where your imagination is capable of producing ideas and expression spontaneously; a state of pleasure from immersion in the activity at hand.

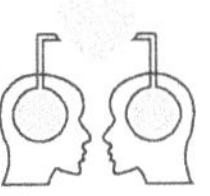

Connectedness

Feeling connected to others, lower defenses and allow companionship; being a part of a team, community, organization, or group.

Exercise 2: Inner Family Drawing

Materials Needed:
Colored pencils or markers (if not available, feel free to use whatever writing medium you have).

Instructions:
Take a moment to center yourself and connect with your inner emotions.
Begin by drawing or creating images that represent the ideal parent, the dominant inner parent, and your inner child. Use colors, shapes, and symbols to express the qualities and characteristics of each inner family member.

As you reflect on your drawing, answer:

How does each parent interact with the inner child?

How does each version of the parents influence your thoughts and behavior?

Write down any insights or emotions that arose from the parenting styles.

Exercise 3: Letter from your Ideal Parent

Find a quiet and comfortable space where you can focus without distractions. Begin by reflecting on the ideal parent within. Write a letter to your inner child, expressing your thoughts, feelings, and desires.

Dear _______________________

Love,

Your Ideal Parent

Exercise 4: Ideal Parent Meditation

This exercise connects you further to the ideal parent (aka Adult or Core Self).
Return to this exercise regularly to strengthen your inner ideal parent. Our
recommendation is to do this meditation daily for 28 days.

- Find a quiet and comfortable space where you can sit or lie down without
  distractions. Close your eyes and take a few deep breaths to center yourself.
- Imagine yourself surrounded by a warm, loving light, feeling safe and suppor-
  ted in this space.
- Begin to visualize the ideal parent figure standing before you. Picture them
  with love and compassion, radiating kindness and warmth.
- Envision this ideal parent embracing you with unconditional love and accep-
  tance. Feel their comforting presence enveloping you.
- Notice any sensations or emotions that arise within you.
- Allow yourself to bask in the warmth of this loving energy, knowing that you
  are deserving of this care and compassion.
- Take a few moments to express gratitude for the presence of your ideal parent
  and the love they have shown you.
- When you are ready, gently bring your awareness back to the present moment.
  Take a few more deep breaths before opening your eyes.
- Carry the feelings of love, support, and encouragement with you as you go
  about the exercises, knowing that you can always return to this visualization
  whenever you need a reminder of your own inner strength and worth. We will
  come back to this exercise when we go through the journal entries, especially
  as we come across tough ones.

Meeting Your Inner Child

A Gentle Introduction to Your Inner Child

As you reconnect with your inner child, remember that the adult self or ideal parent is always there and available to support you. Take a moment to connect to them if you ever feel overwhelmed by an inner child's emotional pain.

Many people find it challenging to recall their childhood, often due to shutting down or dissociating as a coping mechanism for the intense emotional pain. The initial step to reconnect with your inner child is then to do so in a gentle and reassuring way.

Approach your inner wounds with the same tenderness you would offer a new friend. Take time to understand their intricacies, fears, and hopes. Listen to their whispers, honor their presence, and reassure them that they are safe with you.

Remember, trust takes time to build. As you seek to understand your inner child, let them get to know you as well. Understand that they may feel upset after years of neglect and may need time to trust you fully. Be patient and invest in this relationship.

As you connect, walls gradually crumble, and wounds start to heal. With deepening trust comes a greater capacity for healing. Within this gentle ebb and flow, transformation takes root, nourished by acceptance and care.

A gentle reminder: give yourself plenty of breaks and space throughout this process. Healing is not a race to be won but a journey to be embraced with patience and compassion.

Exercise 1: A Gentle Introduction

We will now begin to connect with Your Inner Child (If you can't recall a specific situation or answer a particular question, it's okay; simply move forward).

Reflecting on a cherished memory from your childhood, think back to a moment that brings a smile to your face. What made this memory so special? How did it fill your heart with joy and warmth at the time, and how does it continue to evoke those feelings now?

Recall ONE challenging experience from your childhood—a time when you felt tested, perhaps overwhelmed.

Think back to the activities or hobbies that brought you joy as a child. What were the interests? How did it feel to participate or explore them?

Reflect on the environments of your childhood—the places you called home, the schools you attended, the neighborhoods you roamed. What were the places like? Who were there with you?

Write about any dreams or desires you held dear as a child—visions of the future, aspirations waiting to be realized. What was it like to have them?

Imagine yourself as a child again, sitting in your favorite spot indoor or outdoor. Describe the scene around you using all five senses. What do you see, hear, smell, taste, and feel?

Create a list of your favorite childhood games, toys, or activities. Choose one and write about a vivid memory you have associated with it. How did this activity make you feel at the time, and how does it make you feel now?

Reflect on a time when you felt pure joy and wonder as a child. Describe the experience in detail, focusing on the emotions and sensations you felt in that moment.

Materials Needed: If you have colored pencils or markers, great! If not, use any writing medium you have on hand.

Draw a picture of your inner child as you envision them. What do they look like? What are they wearing? How are they feeling? Let your imagination run wild!

Sketch a scene from your favorite childhood memory. It could be a family vacation, a special celebration, or a quiet moment spent alone. Capture the essence of that memory in your drawing.

Use colors and/or shapes to express your inner child's emotions. Draw a series of abstract doodles or patterns that represent different feelings such as joy, sadness, excitement, or curiosity.

Exercise 2: Childhood Bedroom Visualization

This exercise gently connects you with an inner child's wound that needs your attention at the present moment.

1. Find a comfortable space and set aside quiet, uninterrupted time to connect with your inner child.
2. Close your eyes and take deep breaths.
3. Ground yourself in your present environment and feel your body sensations.
4. When ready, open your eyes and proceed.
5. Set the intention to connect with your inner child.
6. Recall your childhood bedroom and visualize yourself seeing your inner child there. Close your eyes if needed.
7. Answer the following questions.

How old are they?

What are they doing in the bedroom? Where are they located?

What are they feeling?

What memories are they showing you that needs healing?

What did they believe about themselves and life as a result of that experience?
How does that make them feel?

We have now identified a wound to tend to and can begin the healing processing exercises.

Processing Exercises

Overview of Processing Exercises

Healing involves processing tough emotions from the past that were repressed because you didn't have the support or tools during childhood. Our process consists of four steps:

Recall the Memory

Bring the emotional, bodily, or mental memory to the surface to fully understand what is stored in the subconscious.

Acknowledge without Judgment

Love and see the entire stored experience of your inner child. Establish safety by listening to them without judgment. Reassure them that they are no longer in that situation and that you, as their adult self, are committed to protecting and cherishing them.

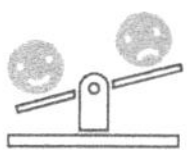

Soothe Uncomfortable Emotions

Hold space for your inner child's uncomfortable emotions, whether they are painful, stuck, or moving. Be patient and commit to soothing all discomfort without the goal of stopping it. Stay with them as long as needed.

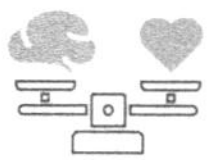

Gain Objective Perspective

Once the emotions have less charge, help your inner child see the situation objectively. Identify any learnings that can help you both move forward in an empowered way.

Learning these four steps is essential. Initially, they may require practice and feel awkward, but with time, they can become second nature and intuitive.

Remember, the intensity of past emotions might have been too much to handle, and you are newly learning how to handle them now.

As these emotions resurface, they may be:

- ○ Intense
- ○ Overwhelming
- ○ Involving body movements (shaking, trembling)
- ○ Accompanied by physical sensations (tightness, heaviness)
- ○ Triggering memories or flashbacks
- ○ Stirring up feelings of fear or anxiety
- ○ Bringing up feelings of sadness or grief
- ○ Causing anger or frustration
- ○ Leading to crying or tears
- ○ Resulting in emotional numbness
- ○ Causing feelings of helplessness or vulnerability
- ○ Accompanied by a sense of relief or release
- ○ Triggering old coping mechanisms (avoidance, distraction)

Commit to seeing, nurturing and soothing your discomforts.
Be patient, gentle, and responsible with yourself.
Take breaks and refer to the emergency toolkit on pages 21-22 as needed.

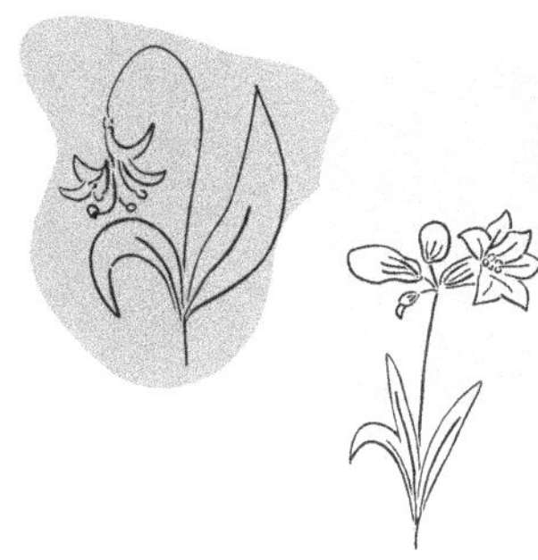

Start Here

The exercises on the following pages incorporate the four steps of the healing process. Think of them as tools. Try each one at least once. You can skip tools, try multiple ones, or use all of them for a given wound. Do what feels right for you in the moment. The appendix contains additional copies of the processing exercises.

As you become familiar with these exercises, you can always refer back to them to process any wound.

You may start with a wounded inner child identified from:

- The "Childhood Bedroom Visualization" exercise on page 40-41
- The Dive Deeper section
- The Timeline on page 94
- Any exercise in this book
- Any trigger, emotion, or wound that feels alive in you

If you are new to this process, we recommend starting with the wound that came up during the "Childhood Bedroom Visualization" exercise.

Healing is not a mental process
Healing is a full body and mind process

Preparation: Connecting to the Wounded Inner Child

Lightly focus on the emotional pain. Visualize the wounded inner child and set the intention to connect. Feel the sensations and emotions in your body, take a few deep breaths, and do your best to answer the following questions.

When is the earliest memory where you felt this way? (your age, the year, the time of year, the month, the day, and the hour?)

Where are you? (As specifically as you can recall)

Who is there? (Specific people)

What is said? (As specifically as you can recall)

What is your experience? (Some combination of body sensations, thoughts, emotions, attitude or mental state, and images from the past) Identify the body sensations, thoughts, emotions, attitude or mental state, and images from the past that are present in this moment?

Exercise 1: Calming and Grounding Breathing Exercise

This exercise helps ground you in the present moment as your adult self. It also soothes your inner child, especially during feelings of overwhelm, anxiety, and emotional pain.

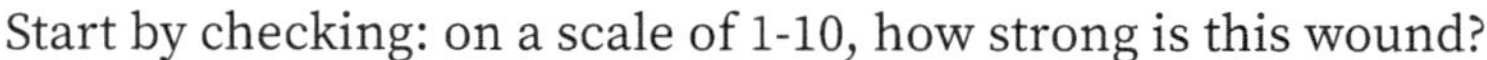

Start by checking: on a scale of 1-10, how strong is this wound?

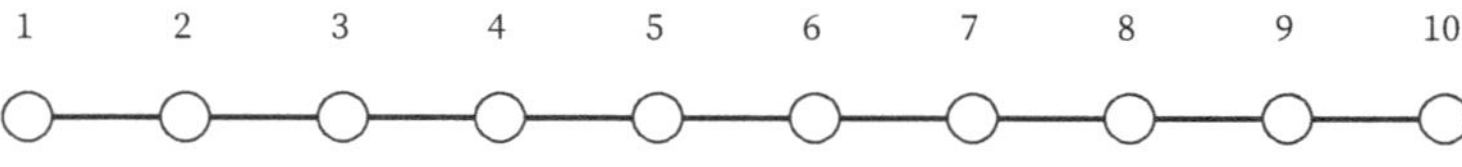

1- Sit or lie down in a comfortable position.

2- Connect with your adult self, who is also the ideal parent within you and feel what that feels like for a moment. Set the intention to lovingly hold space for your wound.

3- Set timer for 3 minutes. You will do a 4-6-8 breathing exercise where you focus on the sensation of your breath as it enters and leaves your body, letting go of any tension or stress with each exhale.

4- Close your eyes and take a deep breath in through your nose for a count of four seconds.

5- Hold your breath for a count of six seconds.

6- Slowly exhale through your nose for a count of eight seconds.

7- Repeat this breathing pattern, allowing your breath to naturally slow and deepen with each repetition.

8- Continue this practice until timer is off or until you feel more relaxed and centered.

9- When you're ready, gently open your eyes and return to your day

Let's check again: on a scale of 1-10, how strong does the wound feel?

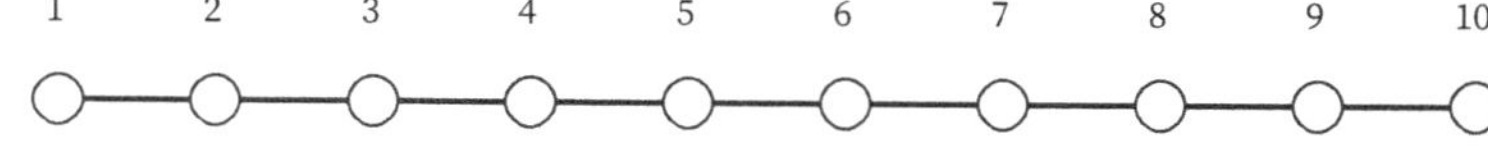

Exercise 2: Inner Child Dialogue Journaling

In this exercise, you will engage in a dialogue with your inner child using your non-dominant hand. Your non-dominant hand is the one you don't usually write with. This technique helps connect with your subconscious and allows your inner child to communicate more freely.

Start by checking: on a scale of 1-10, how strong is this wound?

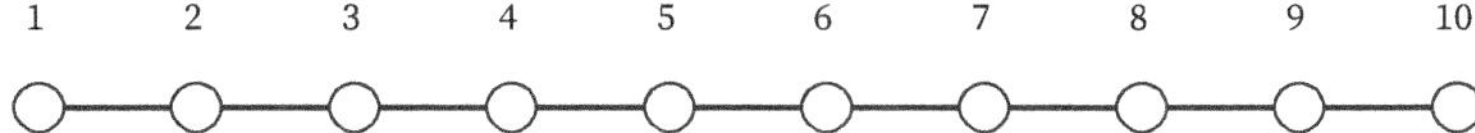

Instructions:

○ Silently or out loud, read the bolded statements below as your Adult Self (Ideal Parent).
○ Write the answers with your **non-dominant hand,** letting your wounded inner child communicate.
○ Note, If your inner child isn't comfortable and says no, take a break and try again later.

"Hello, I'd like to connect with you and spend some time together. Is that okay with you?"

"How are you feeling today?"

"I hear you and fully understand how you're feeling. Is there anything else you want me to know or hear today?"

"Thank you for sharing that. I hear you, and I'm here for you. What you have to say is important to me. I care deeply about how you feel and think. Is there anything else you want to share with me?"

"I hear you. Thank you for sharing that with me. I'm here for you, and I love you. Is there anything you need from me? How can I support you right now?"

"I hear that's what you need from me. Thank you for sharing. I truly hear you and will do my best to be there for you. I love you. Is there anything else you'd like to share before we finish for the day?"

"Thank you for showing up today. I appreciate your presence and trust in me—it means so much. I will do my best to be there for you and your needs. I will come back and connect with you again because you are a priority. I love you."

Take a moment to reflect on the dialogue and any insights or emotions that arose during the exercise.

My inner child is feeling:

I am here to support and care for my inner child. What they need from me is:

I am willing to and commit to supporting my inner child by doing:

Let's check again: on a scale of 1-10, how strong does the wound feel?

1   2   3   4   5   6   7   8   9   10

Exercise 3: Soothing Your Inner Child with a Pillow

Use this exercise to soothe your inner child's distressing emotions, just as you would comfort a child. Refer to it when you feel strong emotions like sadness, anger, anxiety, or hurt.

Start by checking: on a scale of 1-10, how strong is this wound?

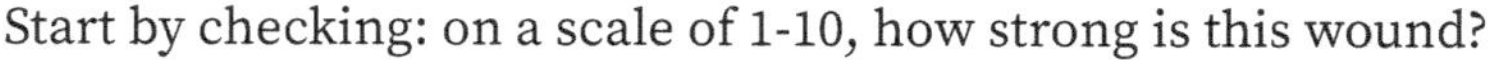
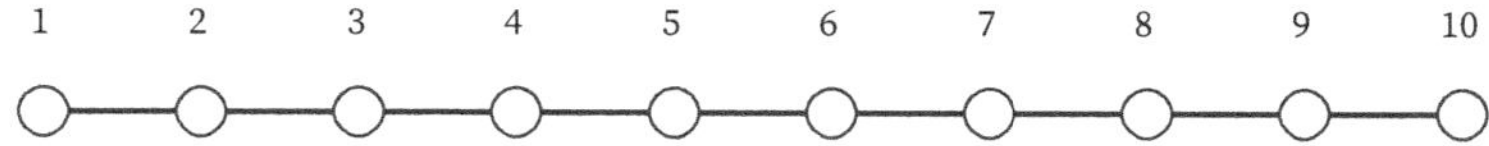

1- Prepare Your Space

○ Find a quiet, comfortable place where you won't be disturbed.

○ Take a pillow to represent your inner child.

2- Visualize Your Inner Child

○ Imagine that the pillow is your inner child who is distressed and in need of comfort. Hold the pillow gently within an arm's length in front of you. Look at it with love and care.

3- Express Love and Reassurance

○ Bring the pillow in closer and hug the pillow tightly, conveying warmth and safety.

○ Begin to speak soothingly and patiently, as you would to a little child. Letting them know:

"Hello, I'm your adult self and I'm here to take care of you.

4- Say the Following Phrases Sincerely

"I love you."

"I'm not going anywhere."

"I'm sorry you had to go through this."

"Please forgive me for not being there for you."

"I'll take care of you. I promise."

"Thank you for giving me a chance."

"I'm here for you now."

5- Be patient and compassionate

○ Take your time with this process. Allow yourself to feel the emotions and let the comforting words sink in.

○ Allow the inner child's feelings and words to surface. Allow them to say what they need to say.

6- Repeat as needed

○ Whenever you feel distressed, return to this practice to provide yourself with the love, care, and safety you need.

Let's check again: on a scale of 1-10, how strong does the wound feel?

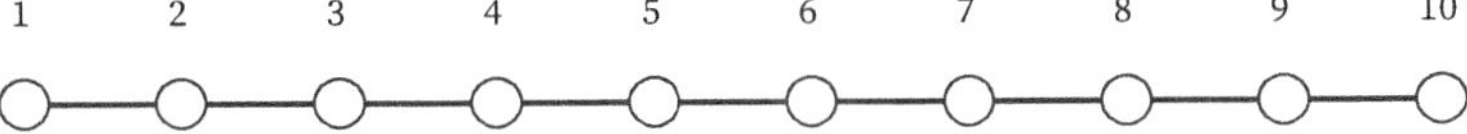

Exercise 4: Letter to Your Inner Child

This exercise helps you deeply connect and communicate with your inner child through a letter.

1. **Connect with the Wound:** Tune in and connect with the wound your inner child has shown you.
2. **Establish Perspective:** Remember that you are the adult self. Ask your inner child to let you see them fully from a slight distance, without blending with you. Picture yourself sitting across from your younger self, holding their hand, and speaking with compassion and understanding. Visualize holding them closer if that feels right for both of you.
3. **Write the Letter:** Compose a heartfelt letter to your inner child. Offer love, reassurance, and support for the wound they experienced. Express words of comfort, wisdom, and gratitude for the resilience they've shown throughout your life.

Start by checking: on a scale of 1-10, how strong is this wound?

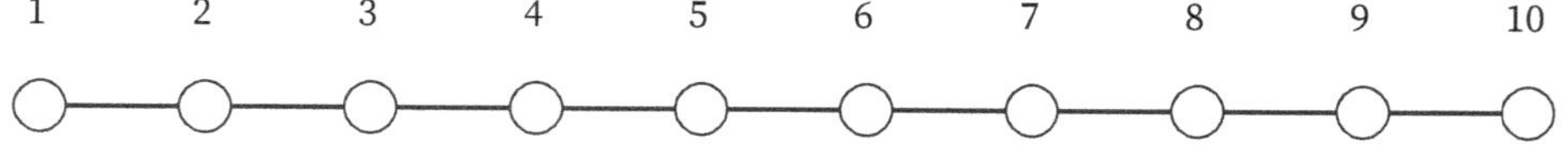

Dear Inner Child,

Love,

Your Adult Self

Imagine your inner child taking in your words. How are they feeling now?

Let's check again: on a scale of 1-10, how strong does the wound feel?

1	2	3	4	5	6	7	8	9	10
○	○	○	○	○	○	○	○	○	○

Exercise 5: Somatic Experiencing Meditation

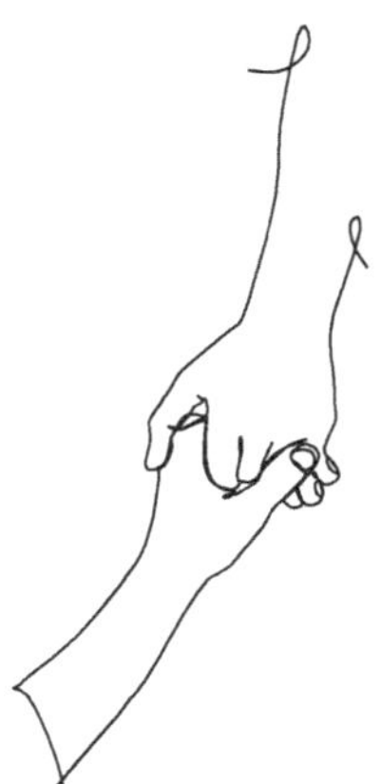

When a child experiences stress or distress, it manifests physically. The intensity is often so overwhelming, and without proper support from those around them, the child learns to repress or ignore the situation. Somatic experiencing helps reconnect with that physical experience, allowing you to fully process it as intended. Animals naturally do this; for example, dogs shake off stress or deer tremble after escaping a lion chase, releasing their tension.

The following exercise is the essence of full healing. You must allow your inner child to safely have their feelings.

Note: Unblending and Parenting:
Practice "unblending" from overwhelming emotions by creating distance and perspective. Imagine yourself as a caring parent to your inner child, offering comfort and guidance during times of distress. If needed. ask the inner child to not take over and to reduce the intensity of the emotions, so you can better support them.

Start by checking: on a scale of 1-10, how strong is this wound?

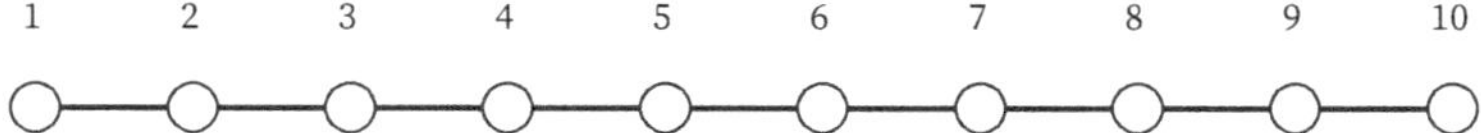

Meditation Exercise:

1- Find a quiet and comfortable space to sit or lie down. Close your eyes, take deep breaths, and scan your body for areas of tension or discomfort.

2- Once you feel ready, turn your attention to what is upsetting you. Focus on one specific body area and observe any thoughts, emotions, or memories that arise. Allow yourself to fully acknowledge and accept whatever emotions, sensations, or images arise.

3- Feel your breath to anchor yourself, while exploring the sensations with curiosity and gentleness. Pay attention to what is happening in your body. Notice any sensations such as tightness, heaviness, or tingling, as well as any emotions or feelings that surface. Stay present with whatever arises and simply witness it without judgment.

4- Embrace what is feeling alive within you. Allow it to flow forth, unfiltered and unbridled. Feel its intensity, let it ignite within you like a flame burning bright. Simply observe these emotions in their entirety as you're also feeling your breath. Hold space for them, offering them the gentle acknowledgment and acceptance they deserve.

5- Direct your attention to the specific body part where you feel the sensation the strongest. Take a few deep breaths into that area and allow yourself to fully feel the sensation.

6- Connect to your adult self and visualize yourself as a nurturing and caring parent to your inner child. Tune to how you want to provide comfort, validation, and healing to the wounded parts of yourself.

7- Ask yourself what this sensation is experiencing and if it is connected to past experiences. Wait and allow any insights or memories that arise without trying to analyze or interpret them. Observe them with love and compassion and allow them to pass.

8- Take a few more deep breaths, allowing yourself to relax and release any tension.

9- Visualize a golden light emanating from a source above you, pouring down and surrounding the feeling with warmth and healing energy.

10- Stay with this visualization for as long as feels comfortable, allowing the golden light to envelop and soothe the sensation.

11- When you are ready, gently open your eyes and return to the present moment, feeling more centered and grounded. Complete the reflection on the next page

Somatic Experiencing Reflection

During the meditation, I felt ________________________ in my body.

The emotions that surfaced were ________________________

____

I noticed sensations in my ________________________ (part of the body).

When I focused on the sensations, I felt ________________________

____

A memory or image that came up was ________________________

____

____

The memory made me feel ________________________

____

As I continued to breathe and observe, I felt ________________________

____

____

A new insight I gained is ________________________

____

Moving forward, I want to remember ________________________

____

I commit to holding space for my inner child's experience. My adult self is
here to support my inner child no matter what. Together, we will navigate
and heal, honoring every emotion and memory that surfaces."

Let's check again: on a scale of 1-10, how strong does the wound feel?

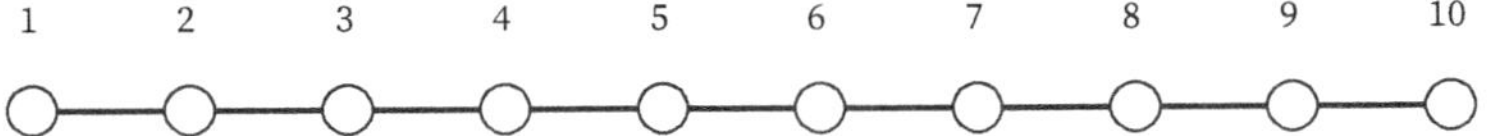

Exercise 6: Integrating Somatic Experiencing and Journaling

Follow these steps when encountering tough emotions or struggling to remember an associated memory. This process helps you recall and understand the experience, hold space for your inner child, and provide reassurance and care.

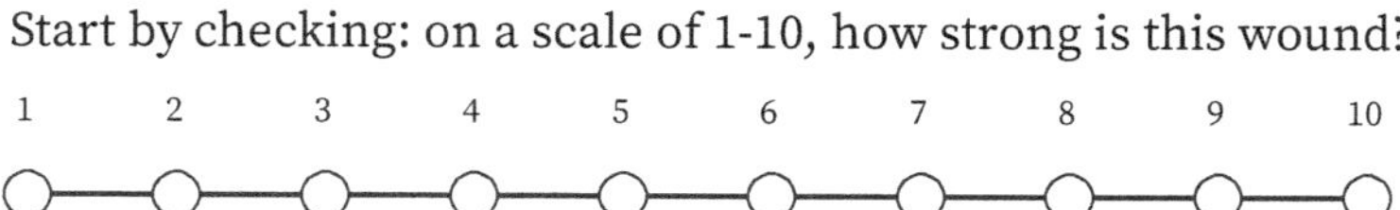

Start by checking: on a scale of 1-10, how strong is this wound?

Step 1: Connect with Your Inner Child

When overwhelmed with emotion, it's your inner child speaking. Pause and connect with them. Ask: What are they feeling? What are the emotions? What are the sensations? Where are they felt in the body?

Step 2: Trace the Feeling to the Origin

Feel the sensations of the emotions and ask: "When was the first time I felt this exact sensation?". Wait patiently. Let any memory or images float up to the surface of your mind naturally. What is the memory or image?

Step 3: Immerse in the Memory

Fully immerse yourself in the memory, experiencing it as if you were there. Allow yourself to feel the intensity of the associated emotions. What emotions are you experiencing? Where are they felt in the body?

Step 4: Nurture Your Inner Child

Step into the role of your Adult Self, who is your Ideal Parent. Acknowledge your inner child's emotional needs and assure them their feelings are valid. Offer them the love and support they deserve. Nurture and soothe their emotional pain. What emotional needs do they have? What feelings of theirs can you acknowledge as valid? What can you say or do to nurture and soothe them right now?

Step 5: Gain Perspective

Only once your inner child truly feel soothed, sit comfortably and take deep breaths. Imagine yourself floating up like a bird from the memory, looking down and observing your the surrounding and people in the scene with detachment. Allow thoughts and emotions to pass through like clouds. Maintain this perspective for a few minutes before returning to ground level and reflecting. What does the memory look like from this perspective? For example, you might see a 27-year-old father losing his temper at a 3-year-old child. How does it feel to view the situation from this perspective?

Step 6: Reflect and Integrate

After gaining perspective, reflect on what you've learned from the process. How has understanding and feeling your emotions helped you? Take a moment to integrate this new awareness into your current life. How can this insight guide you moving forward?

Let's check again: on a scale of 1-10, how strong does the wound feel?

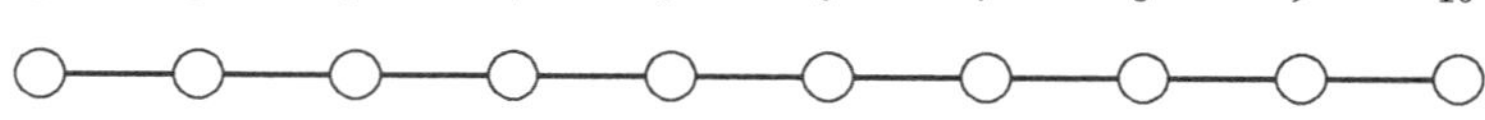

Exercise 7: Ho'oponopono Two-Seat Dialogue

This exercise is based on an ancient Hawaiian healing technique called Ho'oponopono. Use it when you feel overwhelmed, emotionally triggered, or in need of self-compassion and forgiveness. It involves a deep conversation between your inner child and your adult self using four powerful sentences.

Start by checking: on a scale of 1-10, how strong is this wound?

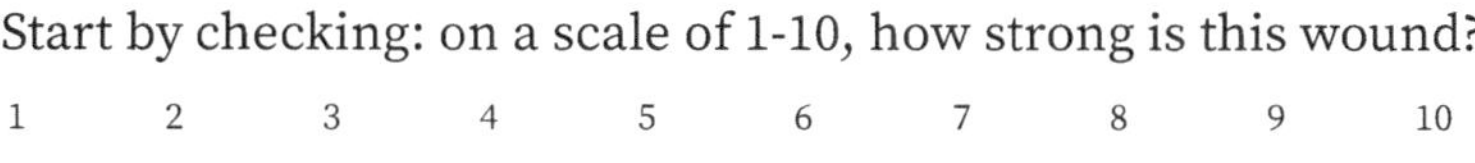

Setup:
○ Find a quiet space and place 2 chairs or cushions facing each other.
○ Designate one as the "Adult Self" seat and the other as the "Inner Child" seat.

Steps:
1. **Sit in the "Adult Self" seat:** Close your eyes and represent your Adult Self or the ideal parent. Let yourself feel whatever comes up.
2. **Visualize:** Look at the empty "Inner Child" seat and picture your inner child sitting there. Notice how you feel.
3. **Speak:** Say to your inner child, "I'm sorry. Please forgive me. I love you. Thank you." Allow yourself to fully feel the emotions that arise.
4. **Move to the "Inner Child" seat:** When seated here, you represent your Inner Child. Feel the emotions that come up from hearing the sentences.
5. **Visualize:** Look at the empty "Adult Self" seat and picture your Adult Self sitting there. Notice how you feel.
6. **Speak:** Say to your Adult Self, "I'm sorry. Please forgive me. I love you. Thank you." Allow yourself to fully feel the emotions that arise.
7. **Repeat:** Move back to the "Adult Self" seat and repeat steps 3-6 at least three more times, taking the time to fully feel every shift.

Use this space to write down any thoughts, feelings, or shifts you experienced during this exercise.

____

____

____

Let's check again: on a scale of 1-10, how strong does the wound feel?

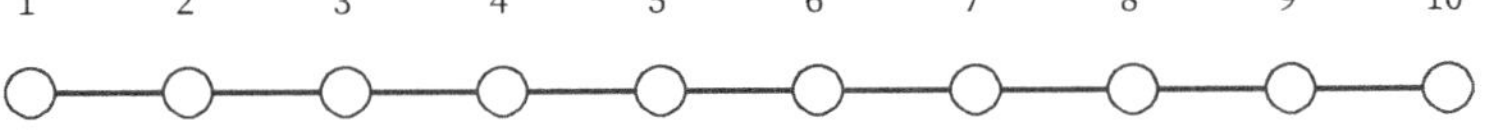

Closing Step: Integration and Moving Forward

Once you've processed the wound, think back to that difficult experience from your past that deeply affected you. Consider the emotions it brought up, the obstacles you faced, and the ways it changed you.

Reflect on your growth since then—how you've become more resilient, understanding, or self-aware. Think about how this experience has shaped who you are and how you view the world.

Embrace the growth and positive changes that have come from overcoming this pain. Remember that every challenge has the potential to teach us something valuable about ourselves and our journey.

In this present moment, feel the safety surrounding you. Embrace the wisdom gained from your journey, allowing it to become a part of you with grace and understanding. With newfound clarity and inner resilience, navigate the world with confidence and wisdom, moving forward empowered and whole.

You want to walk away from your wounds with a clear perspective of what happened and the lessons learned. Aim to feel empowered and better equipped for life while providing safety and love for your inner child. Complete the following prompt for each processed wound.

What are the empowering lessons I take away from this event?

Part 2:
Uncovering Deeper Wounds

Now that we've connected with our adult self and inner child, and learned how to tend to old wounds, we can bring conscious awareness to our deeper wounds.

The following exercises will help you identify these wounds, painting a clearer picture of your emotional journey. If getting in touch with your past pain feels challenging, be gentle with yourself and take breaks as needed.

"The wound is the place where the Light enters you."

-- Rumi

You can complete all the exercises on the following pages or stop as soon as you identify a core wound you'd like to heal. Once you identify a wound to prioritize and heal, go back to one of the Processing Exercises from Part 1 that resonates most with you. If you're unsure, we recommend going through all the exercises of Part 1 in order.

Remember, if you feel overwhelmed, stop and take a break. You can also refer to the "Emergency Toolkit for Emotional Distress" on page 21.

Exercise 1: Reflecting on Your Parents or Caretakers

As a child, which parent or caretaker did you crave love from the most?

Was there a parent or caretaker you felt anger or resentment towards? What did they say or do that made you feel this way?

Who did you have to become to receive love from the parent or caretaker you craved love from the most?

What did you need to do to earn love? ex: get good grades, be thin, be quiet and compliant, etc.

How did my mother feel about being my mother? (Substitute with caretaker if needed)

How did my father feel about being my father?

Exercise 2: Reflecting on Your Past

Describe the environment you grew up in as a child.

What was it like at home? How did you feel at home?

What was it like at school? How did you feel at school?

Did you endure any significant disappointment(s) as a child? If yes, please explain and explore...

What did you make this/these disappointment(s) mean about you, others, and the world?

Exercise 3: Identifying Wounds from Unmet Needs

Children naturally have the following universal needs, although it's common for some of these needs to go unmet. As you read through each core need below, pause and reflect to see if there is a wound from an unmet need.

Core Child Need	Met?(Y/N)	I remember.....	As a result, I feel.....
Safety and Security: A sense of physical and emotional safety.			
Being Seen and Heard: Feeling seen, heard, and validated.			
Love and Affection: Feeling loved and cherished. Receiving care, attention, and nurturing.			
Fun and Pleasure: Engaging in play, joy, and enjoyable activities.			
Support and Encouragement: Being acknowledged and boosted in their self-esteem.			
Acceptance and Belonging: Being accepted for who they are and feeling part of a family or community.			

Deeper Reflection for Wounds from Unmet Needs

I identify with not getting my needs met for:

The earliest I remember feeling this way was when I was about

years old, when the following happened:

As a result, I feel and believe that:

My usual ways of coping with this wound are:

Deeper Reflection for Wounds from Unmet Needs

I identify with not getting my needs met for:

The earliest I remember feeling this way was when I was about
years old, when the following happened:

As a result, I feel and believe that:

My usual ways of coping with this wound are:

Deeper Reflection for Wounds from Unmet Needs

I identify with not getting my needs met for:

The earliest I remember feeling this way was when I was about
years old, when the following happened:

As a result, I feel and believe that:

My usual ways of coping with this wound are:

Deeper Reflection for Wounds from Unmet Needs

I identify with not getting my needs met for:

The earliest I remember feeling this way was when I was about
years old, when the following happened:

As a result, I feel and believe that:

My usual ways of coping with this wound are:

Deeper Reflection for Wounds from Unmet Needs

I identify with not getting my needs met for:

The earliest I remember feeling this way was when I was about
years old, when the following happened:

As a result, I feel and believe that:

My usual ways of coping with this wound are:

Deeper Reflection for Wounds from Unmet Needs

I identify with not getting my needs met for:

The earliest I remember feeling this way was when I was about ___ years old, when the following happened:

As a result, I feel and believe that:

My usual ways of coping with this wound are:

Deeper Reflection for Wounds from Unmet Needs

I identify with not getting my needs met for:

The earliest I remember feeling this way was when I was about
years old, when the following happened:

As a result, I feel and believe that:

My usual ways of coping with this wound are:

Exercise 4: Identifying Wounds from Common Triggers

Past wounds often resurface through various triggers in our daily lives. These triggers act access points to past unprocessed experiences, bringing old emotions to the surface. By identifying these common triggers, you can gain insight into whether certain wounds are present. Reflect on the list below.

If you feel triggered by:	You might need to heal from	Y/N?	When was the last time you experienced this trigger? What happened?
Fear that someone might leave	Feeling abandoned or rejected		
Feedback often feels like criticism to me	Having a caretaker who was critical or disapproving		
I sometimes feel unimportant to those I care about	Dealing with caretakers who were unavailable or self-focused		
Raised voices, certain tones, or certain facial expressions affect me strongly	Growing up in an unpredictable or scary environment		
Loud noises or sensory overload can overwhelm me	Living in chaotic surroundings		

If you feel triggered by:	You might need to heal from	Y/N?	When was the last time you experienced this trigger? What happened?
I don't like being told what to do or feeling controlled	Feeling controlled and unable to express myself		
I struggle with feelings of not being good enough or worthy	Believing I had to perform to earn love		
I often worry about upsetting others	Having harsh or punitive caretakers		
I sometimes feel like I'm a burden to those around me	Feeling like my needs were ignored or shamed		
I find it hard to spend money on myself	Growing up in poverty or with a scarcity mindset		
I sometimes feel dismissed or invalidated by others	Being discouraged from expressing emotions		

Deeper Reflection for Wounds from Common Triggers

I get triggered by:

which is showing me that I might need to heal from:

The earliest I remember feeling this way was when I was about
years old, when the following happened:

As a result, I feel and believe that:

My instinctive reaction to this trigger is typically:

Deeper Reflection for Wounds from Common Triggers

I get triggered by:

which is showing me that I might need to heal from:

The earliest I remember feeling this way was when I was about

years old, when the following happened:

As a result, I feel and believe that:

My instinctive reaction to this trigger is typically:

Deeper Reflection for Wounds from Common Triggers

I get triggered by:

which is showing me that I might need to heal from:

The earliest I remember feeling this way was when I was about
years old, when the following happened:

As a result, I feel and believe that:

My instinctive reaction to this trigger is typically:

Deeper Reflection for Wounds from Common Triggers

I get triggered by:

which is showing me that I might need to heal from:

The earliest I remember feeling this way was when I was about
years old, when the following happened:

As a result, I feel and believe that:

My instinctive reaction to this trigger is typically:

Deeper Reflection for Wounds from Common Triggers

I get triggered by:

which is showing me that I might need to heal from:

The earliest I remember feeling this way was when I was about
years old, when the following happened:

As a result, I feel and believe that:

My instinctive reaction to this trigger is typically:

Deeper Reflection for Wounds from Common Triggers

I get triggered by:

which is showing me that I might need to heal from:

The earliest I remember feeling this way was when I was about
years old, when the following happened:

As a result, I feel and believe that:

My instinctive reaction to this trigger is typically:

Deeper Reflection for Wounds from Common Triggers

I get triggered by:

which is showing me that I might need to heal from:

The earliest I remember feeling this way was when I was about

years old, when the following happened:

As a result, I feel and believe that:

My instinctive reaction to this trigger is typically:

Deeper Reflection for Wounds from Common Triggers

I get triggered by:

which is showing me that I might need to heal from:

The earliest I remember feeling this way was when I was about

years old, when the following happened:

As a result, I feel and believe that:

My instinctive reaction to this trigger is typically:

Exercise 5: Identifying Wounds from Common Limiting Beliefs

Recognizing and acknowledging limiting beliefs is key to healing. These beliefs, often rooted in past experiences, shape how we view ourselves and interact with the world. By identifying these internalized messages, we can understand the wounds behind them and begin to heal. Reflect on each statement and consider if any part of you resonates with it.

There are parts of me that feels:

- ☐ There is something wrong with me.
- ☐ I am unlovable.
- ☐ I am not important.
- ☐ I am unworthy.
- ☐ I am hopeless.
- ☐ I am a failure.
- ☐ I am ugly / never pretty enough.
- ☐ I deserve only bad things.
- ☐ I am helpless / weak.
- ☐ I am unsafe.
- ☐ I deserve to be punished.
- ☐ I am shameful.
- ☐ I am a bad person.
- ☐ I don't deserve love.
- ☐ I have to be perfect.
- ☐ I will never belong.
- ☐ I am unwanted.
- ☐ I am weak.
- ☐ I am powerless.

I most resonate with the limiting belief of:

When I reflect on this belief, I feel the emotions of:

The memories and images that come up are:

This belief impacts my life by:

I most resonate with the limiting belief of:

When I reflect on this belief, I feel the emotions of:

The memories and images that come up are:

This belief impacts my life by:

I most resonate with the limiting belief of:

When I reflect on this belief, I feel the emotions of:

The memories and images that come up are:

This belief impacts my life by:

I most resonate with the limiting belief of:

When I reflect on this belief, I feel the emotions of:

The memories and images that come up are:

This belief impacts my life by:

I most resonate with the limiting belief of:

When I reflect on this belief, I feel the emotions of:

The memories and images that come up are:

This belief impacts my life by:

I most resonate with the limiting belief of:

When I reflect on this belief, I feel the emotions of:

The memories and images that come up are:

This belief impacts my life by:

I most resonate with the limiting belief of:

When I reflect on this belief, I feel the emotions of:

The memories and images that come up are:

This belief impacts my life by:

Review: Timeline Mapping

Review the exercises from Part 2 and place these moments on the timeline, marking each as a blinking red light representing a traumatic event or a crack in your childhood. Add any others that come in mind. You can refer to this as a "Wound Map", that you can use to prioritize or select wounds to process through the exercises in Part 1.

Sample Timeline

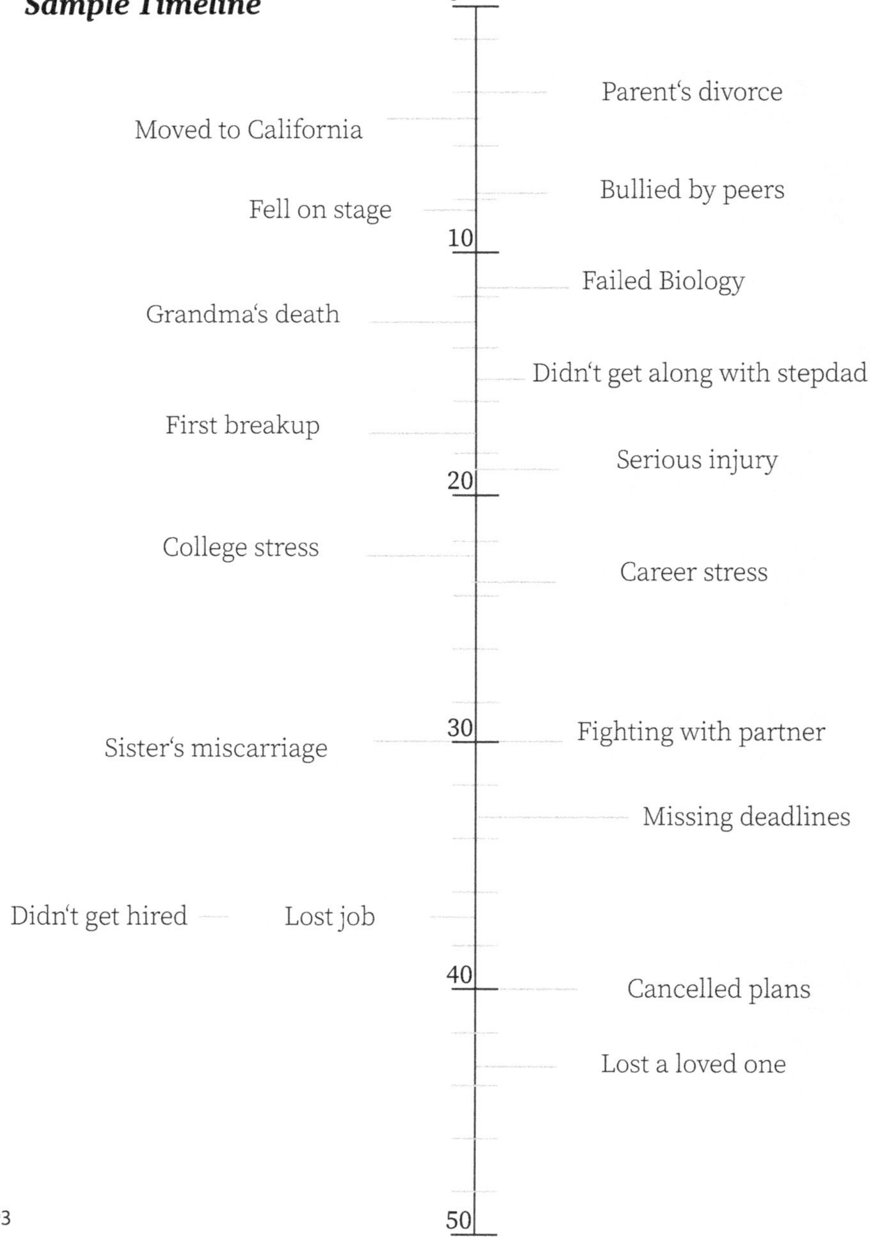

My Timeline

Revisit your notes from Part 2. What other limiting beliefs or core wounds did you adopt as a child that have not been captured?

What were the first moments you adopted this limiting belief or core wound? How old were you? Where were you at? What was going on?

How little or often did you operate out of this limiting belief or core wound today? How does it impact your life today?

Add to the timeline or go back to one of the Processing Exercises from Part 1 that resonates most with you. If you're unsure, we recommend going through all the exercises of Part 1 in order.

Part 3:
Nurturing
Your Inner Child

Exercise 1: Validating Your Inner Child

Seeking validation is a natural part of being human, especially as children. Your inner child looks for this validation from others or the environment. By understanding what your inner child needs, you can provide it directly, helping you make better life decisions.

Read the below statements and answer: What did you long to hear from your parents, partners, friends, or people you were deeply attracted to?

- [ ] You are so special
- [ ] You are wanted
- [ ] You are beautiful
- [ ] You are talented
- [ ] You are valuable
- [ ] You are good enough
- [ ] You make me so proud
- [ ] You are intelligent
- [ ] You deserve my attention
- [ ] I choose you

What did you long for your mother to say to you?

____

____

____

____

____

What did you long for her to see in you or recognize in you?

____

____

____

____

What is something she recognized in you that made you feel loved and wanted?

What did you long for your father to say to you?

What did you long for him to see in you or recognize in you?

What is something he recognized in you that made you feel loved and wanted?

What did you long for your caretaker to say to you?

What did you long for them to see in you or recognize in you?

What is something they recognized in you that made you feel loved and wanted?

Review your answers for this exercise. What are all the validations your inner child long to hear?

Connect with your Adult Self. Imagine them saying all these statements to your inner child. How does that feel?

Repeat these validations to your inner child daily for at least 28 days.

Exercise 2: Cultivating Core Esteem

Every human being has core esteem needs for a healthy psychological self. Sometimes, these needs weren't met in childhood. Review the list below to identify which areas you might need to strengthen in yourself.

◯ I am loved   ◯ I am capable
◯ I am valuable   ◯ I am attractive / beautiful
◯ I am safe and secure   ◯ I am allowed to feel
◯ I am welcomed   ◯ I can do this
◯ I am enough   ◯ I am worthy of respect

Tune in to your inner child and say the statements above, either out loud or quietly to yourself.

How does that feel?

What does your inner child need from you in order to believe the statements?

Repeat these statements to your inner child daily for at least 28 days.

Exercise 3: Active Affirmations

Affirmations are positive statements that reinforce new beliefs. Repeat them regularly—out loud, in writing, or silently—to reprogram your subconscious mind. They are more effective when you support them with evidence in your life. Review the list below and choose one belief that you would like to adopt. Complete the 10-day journaling exercise on the following pages for the chosen belief.

Limiting Belief	Affirmation for New Belief
There is something wrong with me.	I am whole and complete just as I am.
I am unlovable.	I am worthy of love and affection.
I am unimportant.	I am valuable and significant.
I am unworthy.	I am deserving of all good things that come my way.
I am hopeless.	I have hope and faith in my abilities.
I am a failure.	I embrace failure as a stepping stone to success.
I am ugly / never pretty enough.	I radiate beauty and confidence from within.
I deserve only bad things.	I attract positivity and abundance into my life.
I am helpless / weak.	I am strong and capable in facing life's challenges.
I am always unsafe.	I am surrounded by safety and protection.
I deserve to be punished.	I forgive myself and release the need for punishment.
I am shameful.	I release feelings of shame and embrace my worthiness.
I am a bad person.	I am inherently good and worthy of forgiveness.
I don't deserve love.	I am open to receiving and giving love unconditionally.
I have to be perfect.	I accept myself with all my imperfections.
I will never belong.	I belong and am deeply connected to the world around me.
I am unwanted.	I am welcomed and cherished by those who appreciate me.
I am weak.	I am becoming stronger and more resilient every day.
I am powerless.	I reclaim my power and confidently navigate life's journey.

Limiting Belief:

Affirmation for New Belief:

Day 1:

I used to believe   (limiting belief)

I now choose to let go of that belief and embrace that   (affirmation)

Today, I see that   (affirmation)

is true because I found evidence in my life. For example, today, I experienced:

(evidence of new belief)

which confirms that

(affirmation)

Day 2:

I used to believe   (limiting belief)

I now choose to let go of that belief and embrace that   (affirmation)

Today, I see that   (affirmation)

is true because I found evidence in my life. For example, today, I experienced:

(evidence of new belief)

which confirms that

(affirmation)

Day 3:

I used to believe   (limiting belief)

I now choose to let go of that belief and embrace that   (affirmation)

Today, I see that   (affirmation)

is true because I found evidence in my life. For example, today, I experienced:

                              (evidence of new belief)

                                              which confirms that

                        (affirmation)

Day 4:

I used to believe   (limiting belief)

I now choose to let go of that belief and embrace that   (affirmation)

Today, I see that   (affirmation)

is true because I found evidence in my life. For example, today, I experienced:

                              (evidence of new belief)

                                              which confirms that

                        (affirmation)

Day 5:

I used to believe (limiting belief)

I now choose to let go of that belief and embrace that (affirmation)

Today, I see that (affirmation)

is true because I found evidence in my life. For example, today, I experienced:
(evidence of new belief)

which confirms that
(affirmation)

Day 6:

I used to believe (limiting belief)

I now choose to let go of that belief and embrace that (affirmation)

Today, I see that (affirmation)

is true because I found evidence in my life. For example, today, I experienced:
(evidence of new belief)

which confirms that
(affirmation)

Day 7:

I used to believe (limiting belief)

I now choose to let go of that belief and embrace that (affirmation)

Today, I see that (affirmation)

is true because I found evidence in my life. For example, today, I experienced:
(evidence of new belief)

which confirms that
(affirmation)

Day 8:

I used to believe (limiting belief)

I now choose to let go of that belief and embrace that (affirmation)

Today, I see that (affirmation)

is true because I found evidence in my life. For example, today, I experienced:
(evidence of new belief)

which confirms that
(affirmation)

Day 9:

I used to believe _______________________ (limiting belief)

I now choose to let go of that belief and embrace that _______________________ (affirmation)

Today, I see that _______________________ (affirmation)

is true because I found evidence in my life. For example, today, I experienced:
_______________________ (evidence of new belief)

which confirms that
_______________________ (affirmation)

Day 10:

I used to believe _______________________ (limiting belief)

I now choose to let go of that belief and embrace that _______________________ (affirmation)

Today, I see that _______________________ (affirmation)

is true because I found evidence in my life. For example, today, I experienced:
_______________________ (evidence of new belief)

which confirms that
_______________________ (affirmation)

Exercise 4: Fostering Your Radiant Child

The aim of healing the stuck and wounded inner child is to address emotional wounds, allowing you to learn from your experiences, take charge of your life, and move forward with confidence. Recognizing your ability to care for yourself and gain wisdom from life's lessons is crucial for moving ahead with strength and resilience.

Now, let's reconnect with the "Radiant Child," the brighter aspects of your inner child. Remember the brilliant, authentic, and joyful child self that you may have suppressed to protect yourself. Allow this part of you to emerge and shine once again.

"Allow your inner child to play and dance through life and you will stay forever young."

– Lynda Field

Dreams and Aspirations. What did you dream of becoming or doing when you were young? How have these dreams changed over time? How can you incorporate a part of those childhood dreams into your life now?

Playtime and Activities. What activities did you love as a child, especially those that made you feel playful and carefree? How did these activities make you feel? How can you incorporate elements of that playfulness into your adult life now?

Comfort. Think back to objects or places from your childhood that brought you comfort. How have these sources of comfort evolved over time? How can you reintegrate similar elements into your current surroundings to create moments of comfort and nostalgia?

Imaginary Worlds and Creative Project. Recall the imaginary worlds or creative projects you immersed yourself in as a child. How can you reconnect with that boundless creativity now, even in small ways?

Imagine Meeting Your Younger Self. What advice or reassurance would you offer? How you can embody that compassionate guidance in your present life?

Unfulfilled Wishes and Needs. Reflect on any unmet wishes or needs from your childhood. How can you begin to address or fulfill some of these desires now, offering healing and comfort to your inner child?

Childhood Curiosities. Think about the subjects or skills that piqued your curiosity as a child. Is there something you'd like to explore now that aligns with those early interests?

Reconnecting with Inner Child's Playfulness. Recall a recent moment when you felt deeply connected to your inner child's sense of playfulness. What activities or experiences brought about this joy and sense of freedom?

Approaching Life with Childlike Curiosity. Consider times when you approached life with childlike curiosity and innocence. How did this mindset influence your interactions and outcomes? Reflect on the lessons learned from these experiences and how they shaped your perspective."

Materials Needed: If you have colored pencils or markers, great! If not, use any writing medium you have on hand.

Draw a picture of your Radiant Child as you see them in your mind's eye. What do they look like? How are they feeling? What are they wearing? What do they have around them? Feel free to unleash your imagination!

Conclusion

What's Next?

Healing your inner child goes beyond journaling—it's a lifelong commitment to self-discovery and self-care. It involves taking responsibility for nurturing your emotional well-being and developing the skills to parent yourself effectively.

Here are some recommended next steps to support your journey:

1. **Continue the Inner Work:** Remain mindful of your wounds, proactively care for them, and apply the tools and practices outlined in this book. Consistent practice and proactive emotional care are key to your ongoing healing journey.
2. **Seek Professional Support as Needed:** Reach out to a therapist for guidance with deeper emotional wounds. They offer invaluable support and a safe space during challenging times. We have benefited from therapists who are informed in Internal Family Systems, Somatic Experiencing, Compassionate Inquiry, Nervous System Regulation, and Mindfulness practices.
3. **Embrace Compassion**: Lean on your adult self with kindness, patience, and understanding for your inner child. Healing is a gradual process, so acknowledge each step forward. Every bit of progress is meaningful on this lifelong journey.
4. **Practice Self-Care:** Cultivate mindfulness, creativity, and engage in activities that nourish your soul, such as play or spending time in nature. Surround yourself with supportive individuals who uplift and understand you. Celebrate your achievements along the way.

Final Remarks

Congratulations on your courage and resilience. You've taken a significant stride towards reclaiming your inner light and embracing your soul's journey. Remember, you're never alone—supported by the universe, surrounded by love, and guided by your own wisdom.

Healing isn't always simple, but it's an act of profound love and self-compassion. Each tear shed, each wound acknowledged, and each fear faced brings you closer to wholeness. Embrace this sacred journey of the heart, trusting your inner guidance as your soul leads you toward peace and completeness.

You deserve love, joy, and all the blessings life offers.

May your path ahead be graced with insight, peace, and boundless possibilities. May you continue to rediscover the beauty of your soul. We wish you all the best on your bright journey onward.

Hurt people will hurt people." But I rarely hear the opposite,
"Healed people heal people." Get healed. Then, go heal.

-Unknown

Resources

Books:

- "In an Unspoken Voice: How the Body Releases Trauma and Restores Goodness" by Peter A. Levine
- "It Didn't Start with You: How Inherited Family Trauma Shapes Who We Are and How to End the Cycle" by Mark Wolynn
- "No Bad Parts: Healing Trauma and Restoring Wholeness with the Internal Family Systems Model" by Richard C. Schwartz
- "The Body Keeps the Score: Brain, Mind, and Body in the Ilealing of Trauma" by Bessel van der Kolk
- "The Myth of Normal: Illness and Health in an Insane Culture" by Gabor Maté
- "The Polyvagal Theory: Neurophysiological loundations of Limotions, Attachment, Communication, and Self-regulation" by Stephen Porges
- "Waking the Tiger: Healing Trauma" by Peter A. Levine
- "When the Body Says No: Exploring the Stress-Disease Connection" by Gabor Maté

Practices:

- Compassionate Inquiry: Developed by Dr. Gabor Maté, resources available through his website (https://drgabormate.com/compassionate-inquiry/)
- Eye Movement Desensitization and Reprocessing (EMDR): A therapy technique used for treating trauma and PTSD. More information available through the EMDR International Association (https://www.emdria.org/
- Family Constellation: More information available through the International Systemic Constellations Association (htips://www.isca-network.org/)
- Identity Development Institute: Offers resources and support for identity development (http://www.identitydevelopmentinstitute.com/)
- Internal Family Systems (IFS): Resources and workshops from The Center for Self Leadership (https://ifs-institute.com/)
- Polyvagal Institute: More information available through Stephen Porges' Polyvagal Institute (https://www.stephenporges.com/)
- Somatic Experiencing: More information available through the Somatic Experiencing Trauma Institute (https://traumahealing.org/)

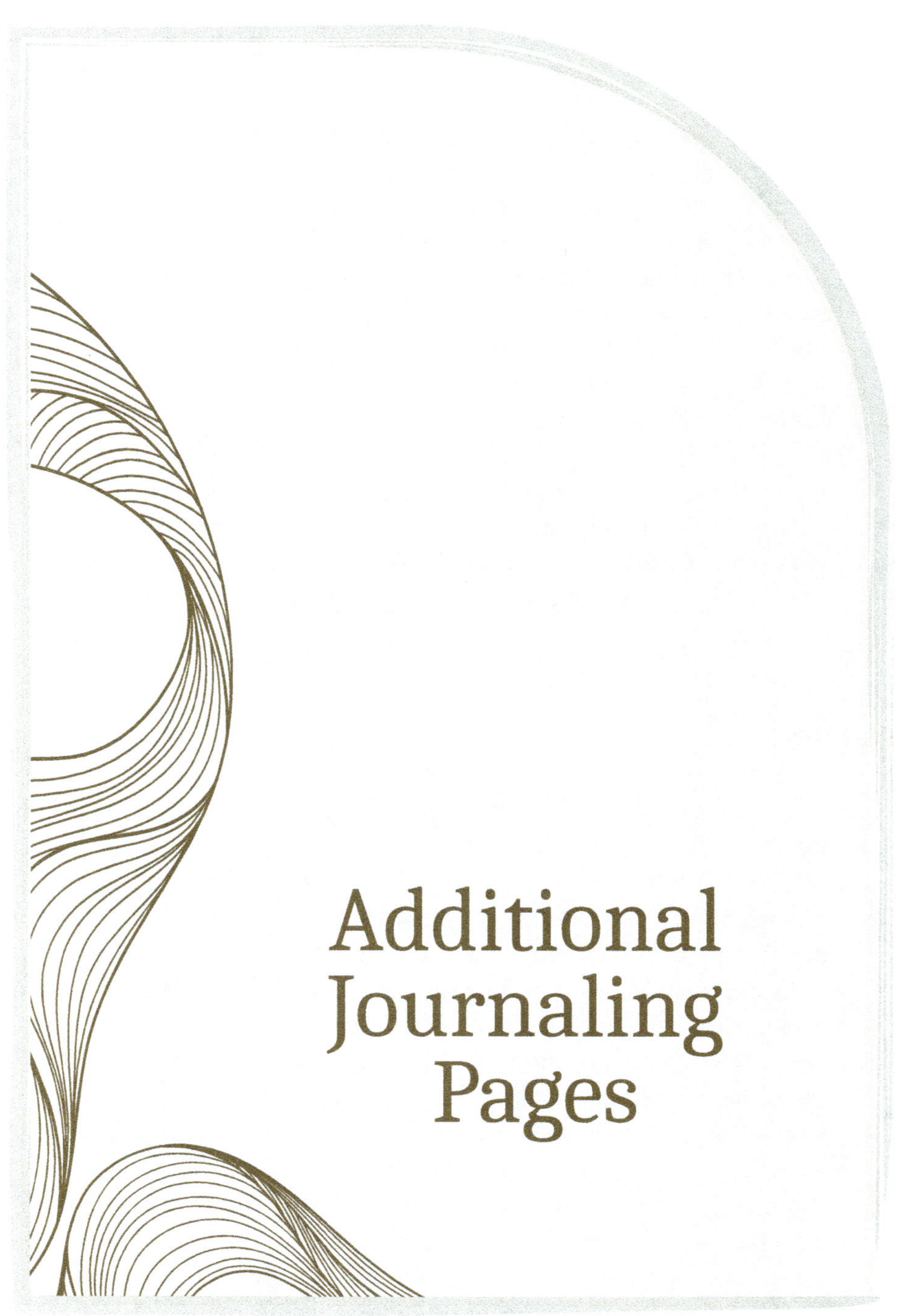

Additional
Journaling
Pages

Part 1, Preparation: Connecting to the Wounded Inner Child

Lightly focus on the emotional pain. Visualize the wounded inner child and set the intention to connect. Feel the sensations and emotions in your body, take a few deep breaths, and do your best to answer the following questions.

When is the earliest memory where you felt this way? (your age, the year, the time of year, the month, the day, and the hour?)

Where are you? (As specifically as you can recall)

Who is there? (Specific people)

What is said? (As specifically as you can recall)

What is your experience? (Some combination of body sensations, thoughts, emotions, attitude or mental state, and images from the past) Identify the body sensations, thoughts, emotions, attitude or mental state, and images from the past that are present in this moment?

Part 1, Preparation: Connecting to the Wounded Inner Child

Lightly focus on the emotional pain. Visualize the wounded inner child and set the intention to connect. Feel the sensations and emotions in your body, take a few deep breaths, and do your best to answer the following questions.

When is the earliest memory where you felt this way? (your age, the year, the time of year, the month, the day, and the hour?)

Where are you? (As specifically as you can recall)

Who is there? (Specific people)

What is said? (As specifically as you can recall)

What is your experience? (Some combination of body sensations, thoughts, emotions, attitude or mental state, and images from the past) Identify the body sensations, thoughts, emotions, attitude or mental state, and images from the past that are present in this moment?

Part 1, Preparation: Connecting to the Wounded Inner Child

Lightly focus on the emotional pain. Visualize the wounded inner child and set the intention to connect. Feel the sensations and emotions in your body, take a few deep breaths, and do your best to answer the following questions.

When is the earliest memory where you felt this way? (your age, the year, the time of year, the month, the day, and the hour?)

Where are you? (As specifically as you can recall)

Who is there? (Specific people)

What is said? (As specifically as you can recall)

What is your experience? (Some combination of body sensations, thoughts, emotions, attitude or mental state, and images from the past) Identify the body sensations, thoughts, emotions, attitude or mental state, and images from the past that are present in this moment?

Part 1, Preparation: Connecting to the Wounded Inner Child

Lightly focus on the emotional pain. Visualize the wounded inner child and set the intention to connect. Feel the sensations and emotions in your body, take a few deep breaths, and do your best to answer the following questions.

When is the earliest memory where you felt this way? (your age, the year, the time of year, the month, the day, and the hour?)

Where are you? (As specifically as you can recall)

Who is there? (Specific people)

What is said? (As specifically as you can recall)

What is your experience? (Some combination of body sensations, thoughts, emotions, attitude or mental state, and images from the past) Identify the body sensations, thoughts, emotions, attitude or mental state, and images from the past that are present in this moment?

Part 1, Preparation: Connecting to the Wounded Inner Child

Lightly focus on the emotional pain. Visualize the wounded inner child and set the intention to connect. Feel the sensations and emotions in your body, take a few deep breaths, and do your best to answer the following questions.

When is the earliest memory where you felt this way? (your age, the year, the time of year, the month, the day, and the hour?)

Where are you? (As specifically as you can recall)

Who is there? (Specific people)

What is said? (As specifically as you can recall)

What is your experience? (Some combination of body sensations, thoughts, emotions, attitude or mental state, and images from the past) Identify the body sensations, thoughts, emotions, attitude or mental state, and images from the past that are present in this moment?

Part 1, Exercise 2: Inner Child Dialogue Journaling

In this exercise, you will engage in a dialogue with your inner child using your non-dominant hand. Your non-dominant hand is the one you don't usually write with. This technique helps connect with your subconscious and allows your inner child to communicate more freely.

Start by checking: on a scale of 1-10, how strong is this wound?

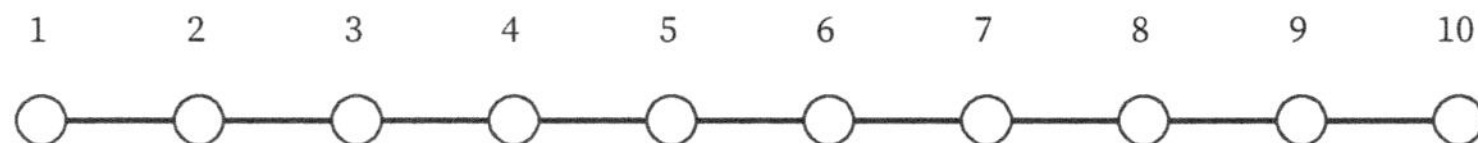

Instructions:

- Silently or out loud, read the bolded statements below as your Adult Self (Ideal Parent).
- Write the answers with your **non-dominant hand,** letting your wounded inner child communicate.
- Note, If your inner child isn't comfortable and says no, take a break and try again later.

"Hello, I'd like to connect with you and spend some time together. Is that okay with you?"

"How are you feeling today?"

"I hear you and fully understand how you're feeling. Is there anything else you want me to know or hear today?"

"Thank you for sharing that. I hear you, and I'm here for you. What you have to say is important to me. I care deeply about how you feel and think. Is there anything else you want to share with me?"

"I hear you. Thank you for sharing that with me. I'm here for you, and I love you. Is there anything you need from me? How can I support you right now?"

"I hear that's what you need from me. Thank you for sharing. I truly hear you and will do my best to be there for you. I love you. Is there anything else you'd like to share before we finish for the day?"

"Thank you for showing up today. I appreciate your presence and trust in me—it means so much. I will do my best to be there for you and your needs. I will come back and connect with you again because you are a priority. I love you."

Take a moment to reflect on the dialogue and any insights or emotions that arose during the exercise.

My inner child is feeling:

I am here to support and care for my inner child. What they need from me is:

I am willing to and commit to supporting my inner child by doing:

Let's check again: on a scale of 1-10, how strong does the wound feel?

1	2	3	4	5	6	7	8	9	10

Part 1, Exercise 2: Inner Child Dialogue Journaling

In this exercise, you will engage in a dialogue with your inner child using your non-dominant hand. Your non-dominant hand is the one you don't usually write with. This technique helps connect with your subconscious and allows your inner child to communicate more freely.

Start by checking: on a scale of 1-10, how strong is this wound?

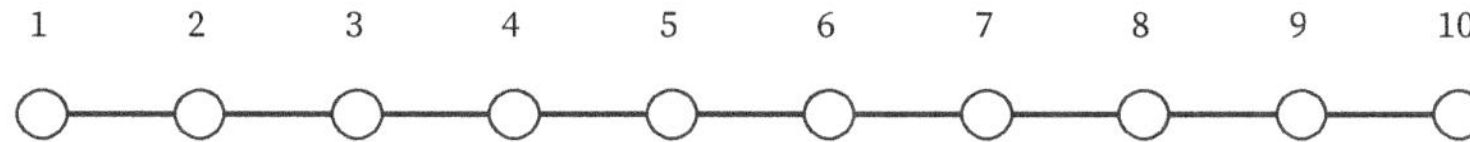

Instructions:

- Silently or out loud, read the bolded statements below as your Adult Self (Ideal Parent).
- Write the answers with your **non-dominant hand,** letting your wounded inner child communicate.
- Note, If your inner child isn't comfortable and says no, take a break and try again later.

"Hello, I'd like to connect with you and spend some time together. Is that okay with you?"

"How are you feeling today?"

"I hear you and fully understand how you're feeling. Is there anything else you want me to know or hear today?"

"Thank you for sharing that. I hear you, and I'm here for you. What you have to say is important to me. I care deeply about how you feel and think. Is there anything else you want to share with me?"

"I hear you. Thank you for sharing that with me. I'm here for you, and I love you. Is there anything you need from me? How can I support you right now?"

"I hear that's what you need from me. Thank you for sharing. I truly hear you and will do my best to be there for you. I love you. Is there anything else you'd like to share before we finish for the day?"

"Thank you for showing up today. I appreciate your presence and trust in me—it means so much. I will do my best to be there for you and your needs. I will come back and connect with you again because you are a priority. I love you."

Take a moment to reflect on the dialogue and any insights or emotions that arose during the exercise.

My inner child is feeling:

I am here to support and care for my inner child. What they need from me is:

I am willing to and commit to supporting my inner child by doing:

Let's check again: on a scale of 1-10, how strong does the wound feel?

1	2	3	4	5	6	7	8	9	10

Part 1, Exercise 4: Letter to Your Inner Child

Dear Inner Child,

Love,

Your Adult Self

Imagine your inner child taking in your words. How are they feeling now?

Part 1, Exercise 4: Letter to Your Inner Child

Dear Inner Child,

Love,

Your Adult Self

Imagine your inner child taking in your words. How are they feeling now?

Part 1, Exercise 4: Letter to Your Inner Child

Dear Inner Child,

Love,

Your Adult Self

Imagine your inner child taking in your words. How are they feeling now?

Dear Inner Child,

Love,

Your Adult Self

Imagine your inner child taking in your words. How are they feeling now?

Part 1, Exercise 5: Somatic Experiencing Reflection

During the meditation, I felt ________________________________ in my body.

The emotions that surfaced were ________________________________

____

I noticed sensations in my ________________________ (part of the body).

When I focused on the sensations, I felt ________________________

____

A memory or image that came up was ____________________________

____

____

The memory made me feel ______________________________________

____

As I continued to breathe and observe, I felt ____________________

____

____

A new insight I gained is ______________________________________

____

____

Moving forward, I want to remember ____________________________

____

I commit to holding space for my inner child's experience. My adult self is here to support my inner child no matter what. Together, we will navigate and heal, honoring every emotion and memory that surfaces."

Part 1, Exercise 5: Somatic Experiencing Reflection

During the meditation, I felt ___________________________ in my body.

The emotions that surfaced were _____________________

____

I noticed sensations in my _____________________ (part of the body).

When I focused on the sensations, I felt _____________________

____

A memory or image that came up was _____________________

____

____

The memory made me feel _____________________

____

As I continued to breathe and observe, I felt _____________________

____

____

A new insight I gained is _____________________

____

____

Moving forward, I want to remember _____________________

____

I commit to holding space for my inner child's experience. My adult self is here to support my inner child no matter what. Together, we will navigate and heal, honoring every emotion and memory that surfaces."

Part 1, Exercise 5: Somatic Experiencing Reflection

During the meditation, I felt ___________________________________ in my body.

The emotions that surfaced were ______________________________________

____

I noticed sensations in my _______________________________ (part of the body).

When I focused on the sensations, I felt ___________________________________

____

A memory or image that came up was ____________________________________

____

____

The memory made me feel ____

____

As I continued to breathe and observe, I felt ______________________________

____

____

A new insight I gained is ____

____

Moving forward, I want to remember _____________________________________

____

I commit to holding space for my inner child's experience. My adult self is here to support my inner child no matter what. Together, we will navigate and heal, honoring every emotion and memory that surfaces."

Part 1, Exercise 5: Somatic Experiencing Reflection

During the meditation, I felt _______________________________ in my body.

The emotions that surfaced were _______________________________

____

I noticed sensations in my _______________________ (part of the body).

When I focused on the sensations, I felt _______________________

____

A memory or image that came up was _______________________

____

____

The memory made me feel _______________________

____

As I continued to breathe and observe, I felt _______________________

____

____

A new insight I gained is _______________________

____

____

Moving forward, I want to remember _______________________

____

I commit to holding space for my inner child's experience. My adult self is here to support my inner child no matter what. Together, we will navigate and heal, honoring every emotion and memory that surfaces."

Part 1, Exercise 5: Somatic Experiencing Reflection

During the meditation, I felt _______________________________ in my body.

The emotions that surfaced were _______________________________

____

I noticed sensations in my _______________________________ (part of the body).

When I focused on the sensations, I felt _______________________________

____

A memory or image that came up was _______________________________

____

____

The memory made me feel _______________________________

____

As I continued to breathe and observe, I felt _______________________________

____

____

A new insight I gained is _______________________________

____

Moving forward, I want to remember _______________________________

____

I commit to holding space for my inner child's experience. My adult self is here to support my inner child no matter what. Together, we will navigate and heal, honoring every emotion and memory that surfaces."

Part 1, Exercise 6: Integrating Somatic Experiencing and Journaling

Follow these steps when encountering tough emotions or struggling to remember an associated memory. This process helps you recall and understand the experience, hold space for your inner child, and provide reassurance and care.

Start by checking: on a scale of 1-10, how strong is this wound?

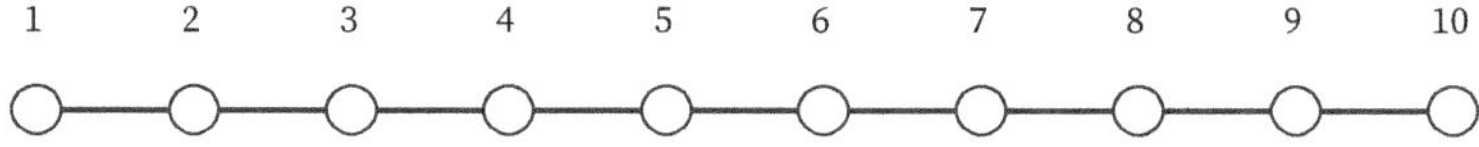

Step 1: Connect with Your Inner Child

When overwhelmed with emotion, it's your inner child speaking. Pause and connect with them. Ask: What are they feeling? What are the emotions? What are the sensations? Where are they felt in the body?

Step 2: Trace the Feeling to the Origin

Feel the sensations of the emotions and ask: "When was the first time I felt this exact sensation?". Wait patiently. Let any memory or images float up to the surface of your mind naturally. What is the memory or image?

Step 3: Immerse in the Memory

Fully immerse yourself in the memory, experiencing it as if you were there. Allow yourself to feel the intensity of the associated emotions. What emotions are you experiencing? Where are they felt in the body?

Step 4: Nurture Your Inner Child

Step into the role of your Adult Self, who is your Ideal Parent. Acknowledge your inner child's emotional needs and assure them their feelings are valid. Offer them the love and support they deserve. Nurture and soothe their emotional pain. What emotional needs do they have? What feelings of theirs can you acknowledge as valid? What can you say or do to nurture and soothe them right now?

Step 5: Gain Perspective

Only once your inner child truly feel soothed, sit comfortably and take deep breaths. Imagine yourself floating up like a bird from the memory, looking down and observing your the surrounding and people in the scene with detachment. Allow thoughts and emotions to pass through like clouds. Maintain this perspective for a few minutes before returning to ground level and reflecting. What does the memory look like from this perspective? For example, you might see a 27-year-old father losing his temper at a 3-year-old child. How does it feel to view the situation from this perspective?

Step 6: Reflect and Integrate

After gaining perspective, reflect on what you've learned from the process. How has understanding and feeling your emotions helped you? Take a moment to integrate this new awareness into your current life. How can this insight guide you moving forward?

Let's check again: on a scale of 1-10, how strong does the wound feel?

Part 1, Exercise 6: Integrating Somatic Experiencing and Journaling

Follow these steps when encountering tough emotions or struggling to remember an associated memory. This process helps you recall and understand the experience, hold space for your inner child, and provide reassurance and care.

Start by checking: on a scale of 1-10, how strong is this wound?

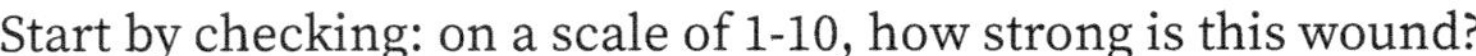
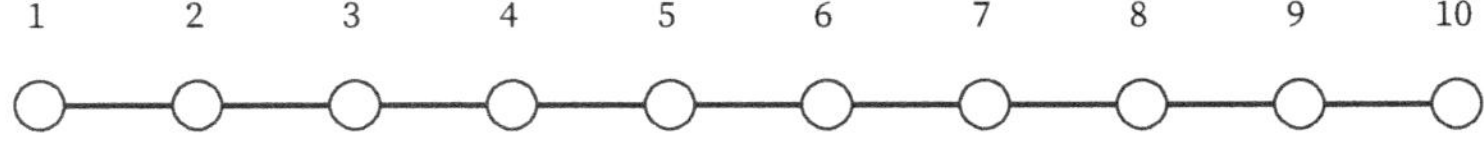

Step 1: Connect with Your Inner Child

When overwhelmed with emotion, it's your inner child speaking. Pause and connect with them. Ask: What are they feeling? What are the emotions? What are the sensations? Where are they felt in the body?

Step 2: Trace the Feeling to the Origin

Feel the sensations of the emotions and ask: "When was the first time I felt this exact sensation?". Wait patiently. Let any memory or images float up to the surface of your mind naturally. What is the memory or image?

Step 3: Immerse in the Memory

Fully immerse yourself in the memory, experiencing it as if you were there. Allow yourself to feel the intensity of the associated emotions. What emotions are you experiencing? Where are they felt in the body?

Step 4: Nurture Your Inner Child

Step into the role of your Adult Self, who is your Ideal Parent. Acknowledge your inner child's emotional needs and assure them their feelings are valid. Offer them the love and support they deserve. Nurture and soothe their emotional pain. What emotional needs do they have? What feelings of theirs can you acknowledge as valid? What can you say or do to nurture and soothe them right now?

Step 5: Gain Perspective

Only once your inner child truly feel soothed, sit comfortably and take deep breaths. Imagine yourself floating up like a bird from the memory, looking down and observing your the surrounding and people in the scene with detachment. Allow thoughts and emotions to pass through like clouds. Maintain this perspective for a few minutes before returning to ground level and reflecting. What does the memory look like from this perspective? For example, you might see a 27-year-old father losing his temper at a 3-year-old child. How does it feel to view the situation from this perspective?

Step 6: Reflect and Integrate

After gaining perspective, reflect on what you've learned from the process. How has understanding and feeling your emotions helped you? Take a moment to integrate this new awareness into your current life. How can this insight guide you moving forward?

Let's check again: on a scale of 1-10, how strong does the wound feel?

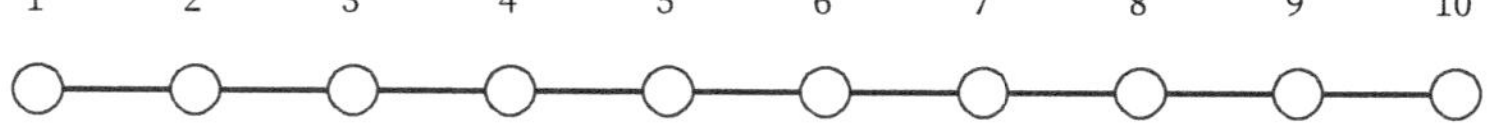

Part 1, Exercise 6: Integrating Somatic Experiencing and Journaling

Follow these steps when encountering tough emotions or struggling to remember an associated memory. This process helps you recall and understand the experience, hold space for your inner child, and provide reassurance and care.

Start by checking: on a scale of 1-10, how strong is this wound?

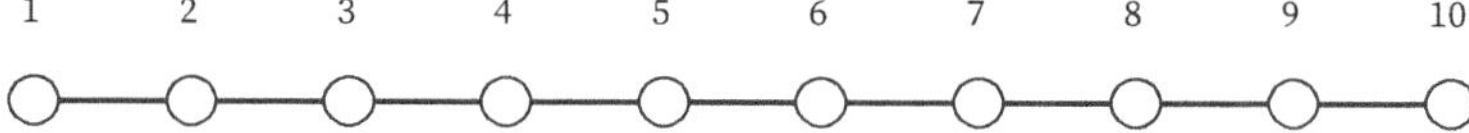

Step 1: Connect with Your Inner Child

When overwhelmed with emotion, it's your inner child speaking. Pause and connect with them. Ask: What are they feeling? What are the emotions? What are the sensations? Where are they felt in the body?

Step 2: Trace the Feeling to the Origin

Feel the sensations of the emotions and ask: "When was the first time I felt this exact sensation?". Wait patiently. Let any memory or images float up to the surface of your mind naturally. What is the memory or image?

Step 3: Immerse in the Memory

Fully immerse yourself in the memory, experiencing it as if you were there. Allow yourself to feel the intensity of the associated emotions. What emotions are you experiencing? Where are they felt in the body?

Step 4: Nurture Your Inner Child

Step into the role of your Adult Self, who is your Ideal Parent. Acknowledge your inner child's emotional needs and assure them their feelings are valid. Offer them the love and support they deserve. Nurture and soothe their emotional pain. What emotional needs do they have? What feelings of theirs can you acknowledge as valid? What can you say or do to nurture and soothe them right now?

Step 5: Gain Perspective

Only once your inner child truly feel soothed, sit comfortably and take deep breaths. Imagine yourself floating up like a bird from the memory, looking down and observing your the surrounding and people in the scene with detachment. Allow thoughts and emotions to pass through like clouds. Maintain this perspective for a few minutes before returning to ground level and reflecting. What does the memory look like from this perspective? For example, you might see a 27-year-old father losing his temper at a 3-year-old child. How does it feel to view the situation from this perspective?

Step 6: Reflect and Integrate

After gaining perspective, reflect on what you've learned from the process. How has understanding and feeling your emotions helped you? Take a moment to integrate this new awareness into your current life. How can this insight guide you moving forward?

Let's check again: on a scale of 1-10, how strong does the wound feel?

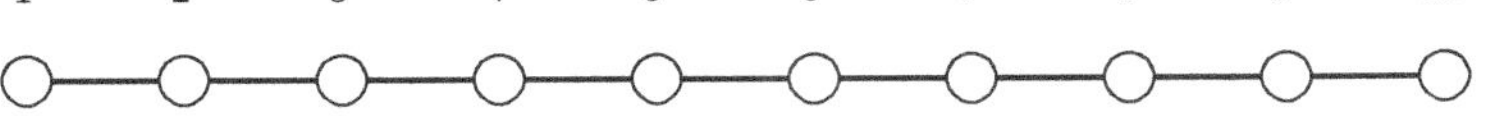

Part 1, Exercise 6: Integrating Somatic Experiencing and Journaling

Follow these steps when encountering tough emotions or struggling to remember an associated memory. This process helps you recall and understand the experience, hold space for your inner child, and provide reassurance and care.

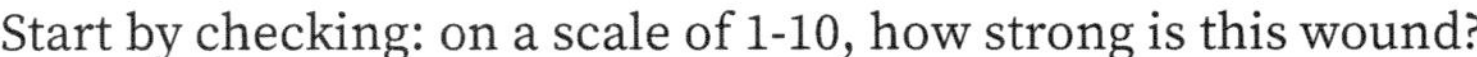

Start by checking: on a scale of 1-10, how strong is this wound?

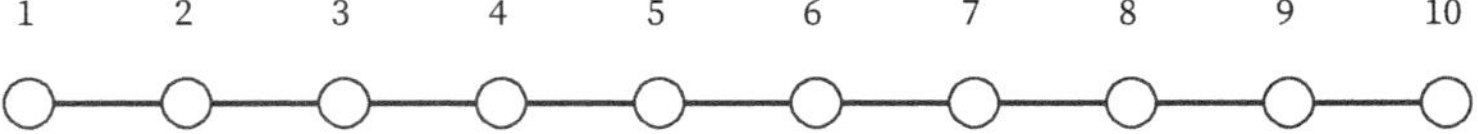

Step 1: Connect with Your Inner Child

When overwhelmed with emotion, it's your inner child speaking. Pause and connect with them. Ask: What are they feeling? What are the emotions? What are the sensations? Where are they felt in the body?

Step 2: Trace the Feeling to the Origin

Feel the sensations of the emotions and ask: "When was the first time I felt this exact sensation?". Wait patiently. Let any memory or images float up to the surface of your mind naturally. What is the memory or image?

Step 3: Immerse in the Memory

Fully immerse yourself in the memory, experiencing it as if you were there. Allow yourself to feel the intensity of the associated emotions. What emotions are you experiencing? Where are they felt in the body?

Step 4: Nurture Your Inner Child

Step into the role of your Adult Self, who is your Ideal Parent. Acknowledge your inner child's emotional needs and assure them their feelings are valid. Offer them the love and support they deserve. Nurture and soothe their emotional pain. What emotional needs do they have? What feelings of theirs can you acknowledge as valid? What can you say or do to nurture and soothe them right now?

Step 5: Gain Perspective

Only once your inner child truly feel soothed, sit comfortably and take deep breaths. Imagine yourself floating up like a bird from the memory, looking down and observing your the surrounding and people in the scene with detachment. Allow thoughts and emotions to pass through like clouds. Maintain this perspective for a few minutes before returning to ground level and reflecting. What does the memory look like from this perspective? For example, you might see a 27-year-old father losing his temper at a 3-year-old child. How does it feel to view the situation from this perspective?

Step 6: Reflect and Integrate

After gaining perspective, reflect on what you've learned from the process. How has understanding and feeling your emotions helped you? Take a moment to integrate this new awareness into your current life. How can this insight guide you moving forward?

Let's check again: on a scale of 1-10, how strong does the wound feel?

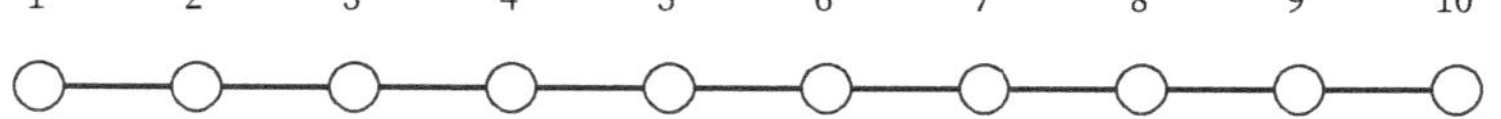

Part 1, Exercise 6: Integrating Somatic Experiencing and Journaling

Follow these steps when encountering tough emotions or struggling to remember an associated memory. This process helps you recall and understand the experience, hold space for your inner child, and provide reassurance and care.

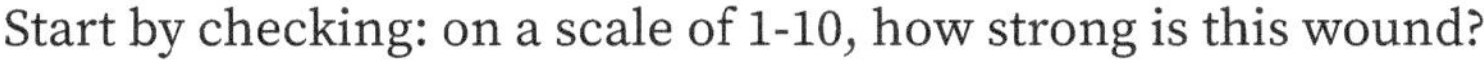

Start by checking: on a scale of 1-10, how strong is this wound?

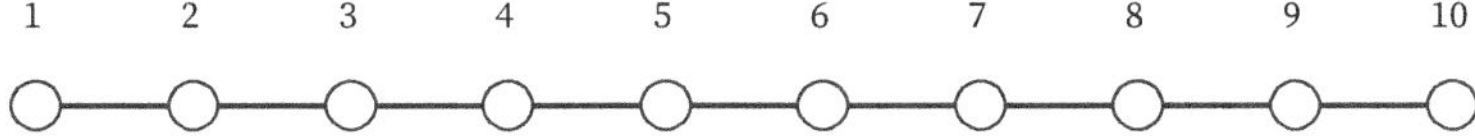

Step 1: Connect with Your Inner Child

When overwhelmed with emotion, it's your inner child speaking. Pause and connect with them. Ask: What are they feeling? What are the emotions? What are the sensations? Where are they felt in the body?

Step 2: Trace the Feeling to the Origin

Feel the sensations of the emotions and ask: "When was the first time I felt this exact sensation?". Wait patiently. Let any memory or images float up to the surface of your mind naturally. What is the memory or image?

Step 3: Immerse in the Memory

Fully immerse yourself in the memory, experiencing it as if you were there. Allow yourself to feel the intensity of the associated emotions. What emotions are you experiencing? Where are they felt in the body?

Step 4: Nurture Your Inner Child

Step into the role of your Adult Self, who is your Ideal Parent. Acknowledge your inner child's emotional needs and assure them their feelings are valid. Offer them the love and support they deserve. Nurture and soothe their emotional pain. What emotional needs do they have? What feelings of theirs can you acknowledge as valid? What can you say or do to nurture and soothe them right now?

Step 5: Gain Perspective

Only once your inner child truly feel soothed, sit comfortably and take deep breaths. Imagine yourself floating up like a bird from the memory, looking down and observing your the surrounding and people in the scene with detachment. Allow thoughts and emotions to pass through like clouds. Maintain this perspective for a few minutes before returning to ground level and reflecting. What does the memory look like from this perspective? For example, you might see a 27-year-old father losing his temper at a 3-year-old child. How does it feel to view the situation from this perspective?

Step 6: Reflect and Integrate

After gaining perspective, reflect on what you've learned from the process. How has understanding and feeling your emotions helped you? Take a moment to integrate this new awareness into your current life. How can this insight guide you moving forward?

Let's check again: on a scale of 1-10, how strong does the wound feel?

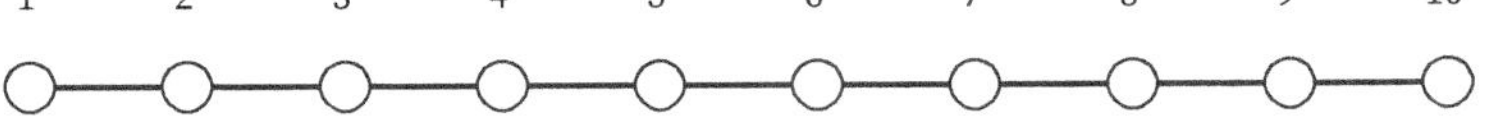

Part 1, Closing Step: Integration and Moving Forward

What are the empowering lessons I take away from this event?

Part 1, Closing Step: Integration and Moving Forward

What are the empowering lessons I take away from this event?

Part 1, Closing Step: Integration and Moving Forward

What are the empowering lessons I take away from this event?

Part 1, Closing Step: Integration and Moving Forward

What are the empowering lessons I take away from this event?

Part 1, Closing Step: Integration and Moving Forward

What are the empowering lessons I take away from this event?

Thank You for Your Support

This journal is our heartfelt effort to be of service.

We would truly love to hear your feedback, requests, and thoughts. Drop us a note on social media @inwardcompanion or email us at inwardcompanion@gmail.com.

If you found this book helpful, please help us spread the word. Write a review, share a picture or video of your journal on TikTok or Instagram, and tag @inwardcompanion.

Send your review or video link to inwardcompanion@gmail.com or @inwardcompanion, and we'll send you special bonus content as a thank you.

Follow @inwardcompanion on Instagram or TikTok, or join our email list to stay updated on new releases and materials.